THE OLDEST STORIES
IN THE WORLD

Theodor H. Gaster was educated at the University of London and at Columbia University. Former Chief of the Hebraic Section of the Library of Congress, he has taught at The Dropsie College, New York University, Columbia, and in 1952 was Fulbright Professor of the History of Religions at the University of Rome. He is the author of *Thespis: Ritual, Myth and Drama in the Ancient Near East* (1950) and is also well known for his *The Dead Sea Scriptures in English Translation* (1956), the first complete translation of these documents.

THE
OLDEST STORIES
IN THE WORLD

Originally Translated and Retold,
with Comments, by

THEODOR H. GASTER

Beacon Press   Boston

Beacon Press books are published under the auspices
of the Unitarian Universalist Association

International Standard Book Number: 0–8070–5787–8

9   8   7

For LOTTA

to tell

and CORINNA

to hear

CONTENTS

CANAANITE STORIES

PREFACE

All over the world and in all ages men have told tales, and many
of these tales have become part and parcel of our cultural tradition. Everyone knows of Cinderella and Snow White, or of the
adventures of Ulysses. Yet the curious thing is that, while the
myths of Greece and Rome and the legends of Indic gods and
Icelandic heroes are "familiar in men's mouths as household
words," the oldest stories of all are virtually unknown. These are
the stories told nearly four thousand years ago by the peoples of
the Near East and written upon clay tablets which have been
found in the ruins of their ancient cities. The reason for their
obscurity is that the tales are of fairly recent discovery and have
not yet fully emerged from the exclusive preserve of the scholar.
The object of this book is to make them available to the "common reader," so that they too may take their rightful place in
literature and popular lore.

What is here offered, however, is neither a bald and mechanical translation nor a loose paraphrase. All stories everywhere
depend just as much on what is implied as on what is said, and
an attempt has therefore been made to recapture, with the aid of
comparative material, that host of ideas and associations which
the tales evoked in their original hearers and which served to
clothe the bare skeleton of words. Moreover, where a story has

come down to us incomplete, an effort has been made to restore what is lost, sometimes on the basis of hints and clews, sometimes from parallels in other lands, and sometimes by sheer intuition. No claim is made, of course, that such supplements are necessarily correct; they are of the same order as the restoration of ancient statues—the alternative is a torso.

The stories in this book are all based on original translations by the author. Some of the literal renderings of the Canaanite and Hittite stories may be found in my *Thespis: Ritual, Myth, and Drama in the Ancient Near East* (New York, 1950). Other technical versions have since appeared in *Ancient Near Eastern Texts Relating to the Old Testament* edited by James B. Pritchard (Princeton, 1950). "Kessi, the Huntsman" and "Master Good and Master Bad," however, appear in *The Oldest Stories in the World* for the first time in English.

The illustrations are taken from seal engravings and rock sculptures made by the very people who originally told and heard these stories. This book may therefore be regarded as a collection of the oldest stories, illustrated by the oldest artists.

Finally, a word about proper names. The Canaanite stories are written in a script which consists entirely of consonants. In several cases, therefore, the exact pronunciation is unknown, and what is here given (e.g., Aqhat, Pabil) is simply a conventional makeshift. Moreover, there are certain sounds in the Semitic languages which cannot be represented in English script without ambiguity or the use of special type. In such instances, I have used a normalized spelling. It should be observed, however, that in such a name as Elhau the *h* really has the value of *ch* in the Scottish word *loch,* while Yassib was actually pronounced Yatseeb. When it is remembered that the Biblical Isaac really conceals the Hebrew Yitzkhaq, the present rough and ready method of transcription will be readily forgiven.

T. H. G.

THE OLDEST STORIES
IN THE WORLD

FOREWORD

The stories which are told in this book are the oldest in the world
—older than anything in the Bible, or than Homer, or than the
epic poems of India. Yet it has been only during the late nineteenth century—in some cases only during the second quarter
of the twentieth—that modern man has known anything about
them. They were composed nearly four thousand years ago by
peoples who lived in the Near East, and they have been recovered from the ruins of ancient cities.

WHO WROTE THE STORIES

The peoples who wrote these stories were the Babylonians and
Assyrians, the Hittites and the Canaanites.

The Babylonians and Assyrians lived in Mesopotamia, in the
southern and northern parts of the country respectively, and they
spoke a language akin to Hebrew and Arabic—that is, a Semitic
tongue. Most of what we know of their literature comes from
the copies and "editions" especially prepared for the library of
King Ashurbanipal, who reigned in the seventh century B.C.
This library was discovered about the middle of the nineteenth
century at Kouyunjik, the site of ancient Nineveh, the later capital
of Assyria, and the tablets on which the stories are inscribed are

now in the British Museum. However, more recent excavations at Ashur and other more ancient cities have brought to light several copies which are as much as a thousand years older.

The Hittites lived in Asia Minor. They spoke a language akin to Sanskrit, Greek, and Latin—that is, an Indo-European tongue. Whence they came originally is at present unknown, but they appear to have overrun the country at some time toward the beginning of the second millennium B.C. However, although they dominated the native populations, they absorbed much of the native religion and culture, and the stories which they have passed down to us derive mainly from two of these peoples—the Hatti and the Hurrians. The latter are the Horites of the Old Testament. The tablets on which the stories are written may be dated roughly between 1600 and 1250 B.C. They come from the state library, which was located at Hattusas, the capital city. This is the modern Boghazköy, about seventy miles east of Ankara, Turkey. The tablets were found in 1906 by a German archaeological expedition, and are now in the National Museum in Berlin. The text of some of them was published only some forty years later.

"Canaanites" is the name given loosely to the Semites who lived in Palestine and Syria before the coming of the Israelites in the thirteenth century B.C. They spoke a language which is virtually early Hebrew, standing in much the same relationship to that of the Old Testament as does the language of Chaucer to modern English. The Canaanite stories come from the temple library of a city named Ugarit, which flourished in the second millennium B.C. This city lies beneath the mound of Ras Shamra (Fennel Head), on the north coast of Syria, facing the promontory of the isle of Cyprus. It has been excavated by French archaeologists since 1929. The tablets, which are now in the Louvre, were written around 1400 B.C., but their contents were traditional and therefore still older.

HOW THE STORIES ARE PRESERVED

All of these ancient documents are written on tablets of baked clay in what is called the cuneiform, or wedge-shaped, script. This consists of horizontal, vertical, and diagonal wedges incised with a three-cornered stick, or "stylus," while the clay was wet. Different combinations of wedges made the various characters.

In the Babylonian, Assyrian, and Hittite form of this writing, each character usually stood for a syllable rather than a letter. Certain signs, however, stood for entire concepts; these are known as "ideograms." The system was derived from the Sumerians, a powerful people who lived in Mesopotamia before the coming of the Semites, and was a conventionalization of what were originally crude pictures.

Different, however, was the variety of cuneiform script employed by the Canaanites. This consisted of only twenty-nine characters, each representing not a syllable but a single consonantal sound. It is thus the oldest alphabet yet known. Whence it came is as yet uncertain. According to some, it was simply a convenient simplification of the cumbrous syllabic script. Others, however, profess to see in it an adaptation to wedge-writing of an alphabet which was the ultimate parent of the more familiar Phoenician script and thence, through Greek and Italic, of our own system.

HOW THE STORIES WERE READ AND TRANSLATED

How the scripts and languages were deciphered is itself a romance. The story of the first attempts to unravel the mysteries of Babylonian and Assyrian has been told so often and so well that it is needless to repeat it. The reader may be referred to the excellent accounts by George A. Barton in his *Archaeology and the Bible* [1] and by Edward Chiera in his *They Wrote on Clay*.[2] The decipherment of Hittite and Canaanite, however, is of far more recent date, and may therefore claim a word.

The Hittites, as we have said, used the same form of writing as the Babylonians and Assyrians. The actual reading of it, therefore, presented no difficulty. The problem was to make out the language, and this was solved in 1916 by a Czech scholar named Bedrich Hrozný. Examining the tablets which the Germans had unearthed some ten years earlier at Boghazköy, Hrozný noticed that one of them contained the puzzling phrase *nu* NINDA-*an ezzateni, watar-ma ekuteni*. In this phrase the only word that was known was NINDA; this represented the common cuneiform sign for "bread." Hrozný argued that since the words *ezzateni* and *ekuteni* both had the same ending, and since this ending corresponded to the suffix of the second personal plural in Indo-European verbs, they might indeed be verbs of mutually complementary sense. Now, a verb connected with "bread" would probably mean "eat"; hence *ezza-* might provisionally be given that meaning, and this conclusion could in turn be supported by the fact that, if the language was indeed Indo-European, the word could be connected at once with the Latin *edo* and the German *essen*, which have precisely that sense. Thus the first clause would denote: "Then you eat (or give to eat) bread." The complement, said Hrozný, would then probably refer to drinking, and the word *watar* immediately suggested "water." In that case, *ekuteni* would have to mean "you drink (or give to drink)," and it so happens that this is indeed the meaning of the verb *ek-* in the Indo-European tongues. Thus Hrozný had established that the language was Indo-European. It then remained but to work out the grammar in detail and to elucidate the vocabulary in the light of the sister languages. The result is that today Hittite can be read with

[1] Philadelphia: American Sunday-School Union, 1916.
[2] Chicago: University of Chicago Press, 1938.

comparative ease, although, to be sure, there are still many words, especially those adopted from the older tongues of Asia Minor, the meaning of which remains uncertain.

The decipherment of Canaanite was a much harder task. Here was a script of which not a single sign was known. Nevertheless, the problem was solved successfully—and in a matter of months —by two scholars, Hans Bauer of Halle, and Edouard Dhorme, then of Jerusalem, who worked independently of each other. The starting point was a recognition of the fact that, since there were only twenty-nine characters, the script was probably alphabetic, and since the city of Ugarit was in the Canaanite area, the language was probably Semitic. Now among the finds of Ras Shamra– Ugarit was an ax-head engraved with a brief inscription which we may represent conventionally as ABC. Bauer and Dhorme noticed that exactly the same combination of signs recurred at the beginning of one of the clay tablets found at the same site; but there it was prefixed with a further sign, which we may represent as X. From this they argued that the clay tablet must be a letter addressed to the owner of the ax, the inscription on the latter being his name or title. Now, Semitic letters usually begin with the formula "To So-and-So." The puzzling initial letter would therefore denote "to," and it was known that in the Canaanite language this was expressed by the prefix L-. Hence, one letter of the script, namely L, had been deciphered! This might seem an unpromising beginning, but Bauer and Dhorme next observed that certain words occurred both with and without an extra sign added to the end, and that this extra sign was variable. They therefore concluded that these extra letters must be the well-known suffixes of Semitic nouns and verbs, and this at once narrowed the range of possible identifications. To one of these characters they provisionally assigned the value M, the suffix of the masculine plural of nouns. Then they found a group which read M-L-? and another which read M-L-?-M. This, they said, might well stand for M-L-K, "king" and M-L-K-M, "kings," in which case K would be added to the known values. Next they discovered two groups reading respectively ?-L-? and ?-L-?-M, where the unknown first and third letters were the same. Now, since this letter never occurred as a prefix or suffix, certain values were automatically ruled out, and there remained only two words in the Semitic vocabulary which would fulfill the necessary conditions—TH-L-TH, "three," and TH-L-TH-M, "thirty." Thus TH had been recovered. Subsequently, by the same process, all the other characters were identified, and the nature of the language, an early form of Hebrew, became immediately apparent.

In order to elucidate that language, recourse was had to what is known as comparative philology. Many of the words were already familiar from the Hebrew Bible, and could be readily translated. Others possessed affinities in Assyro-Babylonian (Akkadian), Arabic, Ethiopic, or other Semitic tongues, so that by careful comparison and combination it was possible to make out their sense. There are a few, however, which still defy elucidation, and that is one of the reasons why certain passages in the Canaanite stories continue to remain obscure.

Yet even when the scripts have been deciphered and the languages translated, another difficulty confronts the interpreter of these ancient texts: most of the tablets on which they are written are either broken or chipped, so that no single story has come down to us complete from beginning to end. Moreover, each story usually ran over several tablets, and it often happens that only a portion of the series has been recovered. Consequently there are large gaps in the sequence, and the correct order of what has been retrieved is often in doubt. Occasionally too, in cases where a number of learned institutions have pooled resources in order to conduct a "dig," the finds have been parceled out among them, with the result that the beginning of a story may lie in one museum or collection, and its continuation in another, while some of the tablets, clandestinely unearthed by natives, find their way into private hands. This, of course, makes the task of assembling the whole so much the harder, especially when long years intervene between the acquisition of a tablet and its publication. The task resembles, in fact, that of putting together a gigantic jigsaw puzzle of which many pieces are still missing.

FORM AND STYLE OF THE STORIES

The stories were designed to be heard rather than read. Given the cumbrousness of the cuneiform script, "books" could not be circulated freely, and reading was something of a specialized art. The tablets were therefore designed only as aids to priests or learned men who recited their contents to the people. Each reciter would, of course, adapt the tale to his particular audience, making additions and omissions at will, and introducing songs at appropriate intervals in order to relieve the tedium. By this process single authorship tended to disappear, and the stories readily acquired the character of anonymous popular lore. It is as such that they have come down to us.

The fact that they were recited rather than read also conditioned their literary form and style. The Babylonian and Canaanite stories are written in verse. Whether the same is true also of the Hittite cannot yet be determined, since we do not know whether Hittite was pronounced exactly as it was written, and therefore we cannot scan it.

That ancient stories should be written in verse is, of course, by no means surprising; verse is easier to memorize than prose. Semitic verse is different, however, from that with which we are familiar from classical and English literature. It is determined not by the number of syllables in a line, nor by the length or shortness of the vowels, but by two other factors. The first is parallelism of phrases. Each verse consists normally of two short

clauses, each saying virtually the same thing in different words—
e.g.:

> The heavens declare the glory of Gód,
> and the firmament showeth his handiwork [3]

Sometimes, however, the second sentence supplements the first,
catching up the idea and extending it—e.g.:

> Who can discern his errors?
> Clear thou me from hidden faults.[4]

The second factor is beat. Each line consists of so many stressed
or accented syllables. In the Babylonian "War of the Gods," for
example, four accents go to a line, and there is usually a caesura,
or break, after the word containing the second:

> When naúght call'd ský   there wás abóve,
> and naúght nam'd eárth   there wás belów.[5]

In Canaanite and Old Testament verse, on the other hand, the
line is usually divided into two halves of three beats each:

> My stréngth and réfuge art Thoú;
> Deláy not, Ó my Gód! [6]

Of course there are variations; no good poet is hidebound. In
"excited" passages, for instance, the verse becomes rapid and
jerky and assumes a staccato effect:

> Now fell Baal, now Mot;
> Now triumph'd Baal, now Mot.[7]

---

[3] Psalm 19:1.
[4] Psalm 19:12.
[5] First Tablet, 1–2.
[6] Psalm 40:17.
[7] "The Story of Baal," I, vi, 21–22.

Similarly, in dirges and laments, the second half of the line contains only two beats, producing a distinctly limping effect:

> Outdoors they lie on the ground,
>   young men and old;
> My youths and maidens all
>   fall by the sword.[8]

From these examples it will be apparent that Semitic verse is governed more by rhythm and cadence than by formal meter, and this, of course, is due to the fact that Semitic poetry was designed primarily for recitation.

Another literary characteristic of these tales is that they are usually related in the present tense, and in the case of the Canaanite documents a special "emphatic" form is often employed, the general effect of which may best be conveyed by such paraphrases as "See, he comes," or "Lo, he speaks." This device is, of course, a very obvious method of increasing dramatic momentum, and all readers of American fiction will recall how effectively it was used for this purpose by Damon Runyon. It is possible, however, that it really goes back to a more primitive age when mythological tales took the form of spoken accompaniments to what was actually being represented in pantomime. As the various characters came upon the stage and went through their appropriate motions, the narrator or "commentator" would describe what they were doing, and, naturally, he would use the present tense—e.g., "Here is Anat coming to the rescue of Baal," or "See Gilgamesh and Enkidu advancing upon the ogre Humbaba," and so forth. The convention then persisted as a feature of popular tales long after the pantomimes themselves had ceased to be performed.

---

[8] Lamentations 2:21.

Clichés and stereotyped formulas also appear. These again are part and parcel of popular tradition. Modern students have long since recognized their presence as a standard element of the average European or American folk tale. The most familiar are, of course, such opening and closing formulas as "Once upon a time" and "They lived happily ever after." But there are others which are scarcely less common: the initial proverb and the concluding moral; the introduction, at appropriate intervals, of rhymes and jingles; the use of such clichés as "the beautiful maiden" and "the handsome prince," or of mechanical and unvaried similes—e.g., "Her eyes were like liquid pearls, and her cheeks were suffused with the tint of roses." Homer, for instance, has a whole stock of standard epithets: Agamemnon is "divine," the sea is "many-murmuring," and dawn is "rosy-fingered"; while in the same way a cardinal element of ancient Scandinavian verse is the employment of "kennings," or stereotyped descriptive phrases, as when battle is "the storm of Odin" or a ship "the steed of the billows."

Devices of the same kind appear in our stories. There too we find a regular use of "kennings," as when Baal is always "Baal Puissant" or "the Rider on the Clouds," Anat always "the Virgin," El (God) always "the Bull, the King," and Asherat "Queen Asherat of the Sea." And there are likewise stereotyped phrases to describe stock situations. In the Canaanite tales nobody speaks without first "lifting his (or her) voice," while the Hittite heroes and heroines rarely "say" but usually "proceed to speak." Similarly, the Hittite gods "put on their swift shoes" when they embark on a journey, while their Canaanite counterparts invariably travel "a thousand acres, ten thousand tracts" in order to reach their destination. At the approach of a suppliant, El (God) "places his foot on the footstool . . . twiddles his fingers and laughs"; and whenever anyone is excited or alarmed, "sweat runs down o'er his face, he quivers in every joint, and his backbone seems nigh to snap." Similarly, when Baal curses his adversary, the genius of sea and stream, he employs exactly the same formula as is again pronounced by King Keret over his upstart son.

Common also is the literary device known in Gaelic tales as the "run," that is, a climactic succession of short, staccato phrases used to describe a consecutive series of related acts—e.g., "They made the hard ground into soft, and the soft into spring wells; they made the rocks into pebbles, and the pebbles into gravel, and the gravel fell over the country like hailstones." [9] When El and Anat mourn for Baal, each of them is said to "come down from the throne and sit upon the footstool, and from the footstool and sit upon the ground." Similarly, when Telipinu, the Hittite god of fertility, departs from mankind, "bull rejects cow, sheep rejects dam," and so on.

Sometimes, too, snatches of song are introduced into the narrative. The original purpose of this was to relieve the monotony of the recital by providing an opportunity for "audience participation"—a technique which likewise underlies the employment of clichés and "runs." The songs were familiar hymns or secular jingles inserted at points where they seemed appropriate or where there was a logical pause in the story. In the Canaanite "Story of Baal," for example, when that god finally gives in to his architect and permits windows to be cut in the walls of his new palace, the architect replies by praising him in the words of a standard hymn, in which, no doubt, the audience joined. In precisely the same way, the Bible embellishes the story of the crossing of the Red Sea by introducing a rousing poem (Exodus 15) which Moses and the children of Israel are then supposed to have sung; while the author of the Book of Jonah makes the prophet spend his time in the belly of the "great fish" singing snatches of psalms!

[9] Quoted from Seumas MacManus's *Donegal Fairy Stories,* by Stith Thompson in *The Folktale* (New York: Dryden Press, 1946), p. 459.

THE BACKGROUND OF THE STORIES

Students of folklore have long since observed that nursery rhymes and nursery games are often but the last lingering survivals of what were originally religious rites. "Eeny, meeny, miny, mo," for example, began as a solemn incantation used for purposes of magic, while Blind Man's Buff and Tag are relics of primitive procedures by which victims were selected for human sacrifice. It is the same with tales. What becomes in time a matter of innocent diversion often started as a serious liturgical myth.

Ancient rituals often took the form of pantomimes or plays, the very performance of which accomplished a functional purpose. Old Year and New Year, Summer and Winter, Rain and Drought, would indulge in a mock combat to determine dominion over the earth. Kings would be married or deposed or put to death, to symbolize in their own experience and "passion" the vicissitudes and rhythms of their peoples' lives. And when these dramatic rites were performed, accompanying chants would be sung or accompanying myths recited, to explain the action and to translate it from the particular into the universal. In course of time, though the rituals and dramas were themselves discarded, the myths survived in their own right and became a quarry of popular lore which poets and artists might mine at will. But the primitive pattern still lingered on; the nature and sequence of the plot and the details of character and action were still determined in large measure by the forgotten exigencies of the primitive rite. Then, in turn, the material would pass into popular lore. Extraneous matter would be introduced, traits and motifs of one myth would be boldly grafted upon another, songs and chants would be inserted to relieve the monotony of recital, and the result would be—what you find in this book.

In reading these stories, therefore, one must remember that

back of their present meaning there may often lie another, more primitive and more surprising. It is here that the comparative method comes to our aid. For the rate of disintegration is not everywhere the same, and by aligning a particular tale with others of the same type it is often possible to recover the successive stages, and thence to work back to the original significance. "The Heavenly Bow," for example, would seem to go back to a seasonal myth designed to explain the barrenness of the earth during the season when the Huntsman disappears from the sky and the Heavenly Bow is no more to be seen. Similarly, "The Snaring of the Dragon," which was recited annually at a late summer festival, appears to be but an ancient version of the familiar mummers' play or seasonal parade, the primary theme of which is to portray the victory of the hero over the dragon of the swollen rivers.

INTERPRETING THE STORIES

It is not easy to retell a story that is three or four thousand years old. Quite apart from the difficulty of translating the ancient languages correctly, there is the task of recovering the background against which the stories were composed. For any good story depends not only on what is actually said but also on what is tacitly implied. The writer or narrator relies perforce upon a mass of popular lore and tradition which his readers or audience readily supply and which covers with flesh the bare skeleton of words. He will say, for example, that the witch took her broomstick, and everyone will know at once that she flew through the air; or he will say that the hero put on his magic boots, and it will be clear that miraculous distances were traversed. Sometimes, indeed, as in the telling of jokes, a mere gesture or a seemingly trivial phrase will convey the meaning. Who, for instance, has ever told a tale without accompanying the "ughs" and "ohs" with a facial expression? And who, in our day, would fail to understand what was meant by "a frock-coat-and-striped-pants type of man" or by "the steely glance of a suspicious bank manager"?

But three or four thousand years is a long time, and during the interval most of the background and "atmosphere" has receded into oblivion. Only the bare words of the ancient stories have come down to us, and however accurately they are translated, they convey but a portion of the sense.

How, then, can we make up the other portion? One way, of course, is to cast about in other departments of ancient literature for scraps and tidbits of information that may clarify what is obscure in the tales. Sometimes, that is to say, a seemingly unexciting business contract or a dull and monotonous historical record will recover to us a custom or tradition which illumines some puzzling incident in a tale. Recently, for example, it has been discovered from legal records that, in the area where the patriarch Jacob is supposed to have lived, it was the law at the time that anyone who claimed the prime share of an estate had to hold possession of the household gods before he could sustain his claim. This at once explains the Biblical story which relates that when Jacob fled from his father-in-law Laban, Rachel insisted that he steal the household idols and take them with him.

There is, however, another way of bridging the gap. Tales which are told in one place are often told also in another, and there is a vast body of primitive ideas and superstitions which are the common property of man and are by no means confined to a single area. Whether this phenomenon is due to migration and diffusion, or solely to the fact that peoples at the same level of culture are apt to think in the same way, is a point which is still debated; in all probability both processes come into play, and neither excludes the other. Be the explanation what it may, however, the bare fact cannot be denied, and it provides us with just the tool we need. For not infrequently traits and details of a story which may lack explanation in a particular setting become instantly clear and lucid when they are brought into line with comparable material from other areas, where the meaning and context has been preserved. Or again, by relating a particular story to its generic "type," a framework of common ideas may be recovered into which particular instances, in themselves obscure, may be readily fitted.

When, for example, we read in the story of Gilgamesh that the hero Enkidu complained about a door's having injured his hand at the moment when he and his comrade approached the ogre of the forest, it is not difficult for the student of comparative lore to see at once that underlying this otherwise inexplicable incident is the widespread notion of the magic door which swings automatically upon anyone who encroaches on a forbidden domain. Similarly, when we are told in the story of Kessi the Huntsman that his mother gave him a skein of blue wool when she sent him for the second time on the perilous journey to the hills, we may recognize at once the familiar and virtually universal belief that blue protects against demons ("Something old, something new; something borrowed, something *blue*"). Or again, when God fashions an image out of mud as part of the device whereby he cures the ailing King Keret, the student of folklore immediately recognizes in the episode the well-known process of *envoûtement* (see p. 207).

To be sure, the comparative method has its dangers. One may often call snap in the wrong place, or force interpretations unduly, or be seduced by similarities more apparent than real. One may, in fact, read more *into* a text than *out of* it. Yet, in the final analysis, this is a danger inherent in the very relation between writer and reader or artist and public; it is simply the price of communication, the tyranny of words, and the snare of form. For the appreciation of all art entails, in the last resort, a process of collaboration. The artist has perforce to rely on the sympathy and experience of his audience to transcend the limitations of his expression and capture the essence of his vision; and their experience may often be different from his own, and the associations which they interpose may do more to obscure than to illumine. One has but to listen to a group of persons discussing a book or play or picture to see how the same work may receive a dozen interpretations or strike a dozen variant responses. Multiply this incident by the number of readers of every book and by the number of viewers of every picture or play, and one sees at once that the pitfall of subjective distortion is by no means exclusive with the comparative approach but is the natural toll of all expression. One recalls, indeed, the efforts which have been made in our own time by such poets as Joyce or Empson or Barker, and likewise by the Symbolist painters, to bridge the gap between concept and expression by modifications of words and forms designed to enlarge the framework of association. This effort is simply the reverse of the coin—the inevitable frustration of the artist when he reaches the tollgate.

It may be said also that while the comparative method may possibly tint the stories with false colors, a purely literal and verbal approach runs the equally serious, if less obvious, risk of reducing genuine shades and hues to a dull and misleading black and white.

In the following pages there is appended to each story a body of material, drawn from comparative sources, which may serve to supply a general background and to clarify one or another incident in a tale, or, indeed, some basic feature of the plot. In these commentaries, numbers in parentheses are supplied, which refer to entries in Stith Thompson's standard *Motif-Index of Folk Literature* (FF Communications, 106–109, 116–17; Indiana University Studies, 106–12; Helsinki-Bloomington, 1932–36), where further literature is often cited. The purpose of the notes is, in a word, to place the modern reader, so far as possible, in the same position as were the original hearers of the tales—that is, to enable him to grasp the allusions and to understand at once what may best be described as the "gestures" of word and phrase.

BABYLONIAN
STORIES

I

THE ADVENTURES
OF GILGAMESH

Once upon a time there lived in the city of Erech a great and terrible being whose name was Gilgamesh. Two-thirds of him were god, and only one-third was human. He was the mightiest warrior in the whole of the East; none could match him in combat, nor could anyone's spear prevail against him. Because of his power and strength all the people of Erech were brought beneath his sway, and he ruled them with an iron hand, seizing youths for his service and taking to himself any maiden he wished.

At length they could endure it no longer, and prayed to heaven for relief. The lord of heaven heard their prayer and summoned the goddess Aruru—that same goddess who, in olden times, had fashioned man out of clay.

"Go," said he, "and mold out of clay a being who will prove the equal of this tyrant, and let him fight with him and beat him, that the people may have relief."

Thereupon the goddess wetted her hands and, taking clay from the ground, kneaded it into a monstrous creature, whom she named Enkidu. Fierce he was, like the god of battle, and his whole body was covered with hair. His tresses hung long like a woman's, and he was clothed in skins. All day long he roamed with the beasts of the field, and like them he fed on grass and herbs and drank from the brooks.

But no one in Erech yet knew that he existed.

One day a huntsman who had gone out trapping noticed the strange creature refreshing himself beside the herds at the fountain. The mere sight was sufficient to turn the huntsman pale. His face drawn and haggard, his heart pounding and thumping, he rushed home in terror, screaming with dismay.

The next day he went out again into the fields to continue his trapping, only to find that all the pits he had dug had been filled in and all the snares he had lain torn up, and there was Enkidu himself releasing the captured beasts from the toils!

On the third day, when the same thing happened once more, the huntsman went and consulted his father. The latter advised him to go to Erech and report the matter to Gilgamesh.

When Gilgamesh heard what had happened, and learned of the wild creature who was interfering with the labors of his subjects, he instructed the huntsman to choose a girl from the streets and take her with him to the place where the cattle drank. When Enkidu came thither for water she was to strip off her clothing and entice him with her charms. Once he embraced her the animals would recognize that he was not of their kind, and they would immediately forsake him. Thus he would be drawn into the world of men and be forced to give up his savage ways.

The huntsman did as he was ordered and, after three

days' journey, arrived with the girl at the place where the cattle drank. For two days they sat and waited. On the third day, sure enough, the strange and savage creature came down with the herd for water. As soon as she caught sight of him the girl stripped off her clothing and revealed her charms. The monster was enraptured and clasped her wildly to his breast and embraced her.

For a whole week he dallied with her, until at last, sated with her charms, he rose to rejoin the herd. But the hinds and gazelles knew him no more for one of their own, and when he approached them they shied away and scampered off. Enkidu tried to run after them, but even as he ran he felt his legs begin to drag and his limbs grow taut, and all of a sudden he became aware that he was no longer a beast but had become a man.

Faint and out of breath, he turned back to the girl. But now it was a changed being who sat at her feet, gazing up into her eyes and hanging intently upon her lips.

Presently she turned toward him. "Enkidu," she said softly, "you have grown handsome as a god. Why should you go on roving with the beasts? Come, let me take you to Erech, the broad city of men. Let me take you to the gleaming temple where the god and goddess sit enthroned. It is there, by the way, that Gilgamesh is rampaging like a bull, holding the people at his mercy."

At these words Enkidu was overjoyed; for, now that he was no longer a beast, he longed for the converse and companionship of men.

"Lead on," said he, "to the city of Erech, to the gleaming temple of the god and goddess. As for Gilgamesh and his rampaging, I will soon alter that. I will fling a challenge in his face and dare him, and show him, once for all, that country lads are no weaklings!"

It was New Year's Eve when they reached the city, and the high point of the festival had now arrived, the moment when the king was to be led to the temple to play the role of bridegroom in a holy marriage with the goddess. The streets were lined with festive throngs, and everywhere the cries of young revelers rang out, piercing the air and keeping their elders from sleep. Suddenly, above the din and hubbub, came a sound of tinkling cymbals and the faint echo of distant flutes. Louder and louder it grew, until at last, around a bend in the road, the great procession wound into sight, with Gilgamesh himself the central figure in its midst. Along the street and into the courtyard of the temple it wove its way. Then it came to a halt, and Gilgamesh strode forward.

But even as he was about to pass within there was a sudden movement in the crowd, and a moment later Enkidu was seen standing in front of the gleaming doors, shouting defiance and barring the way with his foot.

The crowd shrank back amazed, but their amazement was tempered with a secret relief.

"Now at last," each whispered to his neighbor, "Gilgamesh has met his match. Why, this man is his living image! A trifle shorter, perhaps, but just as strong, for he was weaned on the milk of wild beasts! Now we shall see things humming in Erech!"

Gilgamesh, however, was by no means dismayed; for he had been forewarned in dreams of what was about to take place. He had dreamed that he was standing under the stars when suddenly there had fallen upon him from heaven a massive bolt which he could not remove. And then he had dreamed that a huge mysterious ax had suddenly been hurled into the center of the city, no man knew whence. He had related these dreams to his mother, and she had told him that they presaged the arrival of a mighty man whom he would not be able to resist but who would in time become his closest friend.

Gilgamesh strode forward to meet his opponent, and in a few moments they were locked in battle, raging and butting like bulls. At last Gilgamesh sank to the ground and knew that he had indeed met his match.

But Enkidu was chivalrous as well as strong, and saw at once that his opponent was not simply a blustering tyrant, as he had been led to believe, but a brave and stout-hearted warrior, who had courageously accepted his challenge and not flinched from the fight.

"Gilgamesh," said he, "you have proved full well that you are the child of a goddess and that heaven itself has set you on your throne. I shall no longer oppose you. Let us be friends."

And, raising him to his feet, he embraced him.

Now Gilgamesh loved adventure and could never resist a hazard. One day he proposed to Enkidu that they go together into the mountains and, as an act of daring, cut down one of the cedars in the sacred forest of the gods.

"That is not easy," replied his friend, "for the forest is guarded by a fierce and terrible monster called Humbaba.

Often, when I lived with the beasts, I beheld his works. His voice is a whirlwind, and he snorts fire, and his breath is the plague."

"For shame!" retorted Gilgamesh. "Should a brave warrior like you be frightened of battle? Only the gods can escape death; and how will you face your children when they ask you what you did in the day when Gilgamesh fell?"

Then Enkidu was persuaded, and, after weapons and axes had been fashioned, Gilgamesh went to the elders of the city and told them of his plan. They warned him against it, but he refused to yield, and promptly repaired to the sun-god and implored his aid. The sun-god, however, was reluctant to help him. So Gilgamesh turned to his mother, the heavenly queen Ninsun, and begged her to intervene. But when she heard of his plan she too was filled with dismay.

Putting on her finest raiment and her crown, she went up to the roof of the temple and addressed the sun-god. "Sun-God," she said, "you are the god of justice. Why, then, have you allowed me to bear this son, yet made him so restless and wild? Now, dear Sun-God, he has taken it into his head to travel for days on long and perilous paths only to do battle with the monster Humbaba! I beg you to watch over him day and night, and to bring him back to me safe and sound!"

When the sun-god saw her tears, his heart melted with compassion and he promised to help the heroes.

Then the goddess came down from the roof and placed upon Enkidu the sacred badge which all her votaries were wont to wear. "From now on," said she, "you are one of my wards. Go forth unafraid and lead Gilgamesh to the mountain!"

When the elders of the city saw that Enkidu was wearing the sacred badge, they relented of their previous counsel and gave Gilgamesh their blessing.

"Since," they said, "Enkidu is now a ward of the goddess, we will safely entrust our king to his keeping."

Eagerly and impetuously the two stalwarts set out on their journey, covering in three days the distance of six weeks' march. At length they came to a dense forest, and at the entrance of the forest there was a huge door. Enkidu pushed it open a trifle and peered within.

"Hurry," he whispered, beckoning to his companion, "and we can take him by surprise. Whenever he wanders abroad Humbaba always bundles himself up in seven layers of garments. Now he is sitting wearing only his vest. We can get him before he goes out!"

But even as he spoke the huge door swung upon its hinges and slammed shut, crushing his hand.

For twelve days Enkidu lay writhing in anguish, and all the while kept imploring his comrade to give up the wild adventure. But Gilgamesh refused to pay heed to his words.

"Are we such puny weaklings," he cried, "as to be put out by the first mishap? We have traveled a long way. Shall we now turn back defeated? For shame! Your wounds will soon be healed; and if we cannot engage the monster in his house, let us wait for him in the thicket!"

So on they went to the forest and at last they reached the Mountain of Cedars itself—that high and towering mountain on the summit of which the gods held session. Fatigued by the long journey, they lay down beneath the shade of the trees and were soon asleep.

But in the middle of the night Gilgamesh suddenly awoke with a start. "Did you wake me?" he called to his companion. "If not, it must have been the force of my dream. For I dreamed that a mountain was toppling upon me, when all of a sudden there appeared before me the most handsome man in all the world, and he dragged me out from under the weight and raised me to my feet."

"Friend," replied Enkidu, "your dream is an omen, for the mountain which you saw is yon monstrous Humbaba. Now it is clear that even if he falls upon us we shall escape and win!"

Then they turned upon their sides, and sleep fell on them once more. But this time it was Enkidu who woke suddenly with a start.

"Did you wake me?" he called to his companion. "If not, it must have been the force of my dream. For I dreamed that the sky rumbled and the earth shook, and the day grew black and darkness fell, and lightning flashed and a fire blazed, and death poured down. And then, all of a sudden, the glare faded and the fire went out and the sparks which had fallen turned to ashes."

Gilgamesh knew full well that the dream portended ill for his friend. Nevertheless he encouraged him not to give up; and presently they had risen and were deep in the forest.

Then Gilgamesh grasped his ax and felled one of the sacred cedars. The tree fell to earth with a loud crash, and out rushed Humbaba from his house, growling and roaring.

Now the monster had a strange and terrible face, with one eye in the middle, which could turn to stone any upon whom it gazed. As he came storming through the thicket, nearer and nearer, and as the tearing and cracking of branches announced his approach, Gilgamesh for the first time grew truly frightened.

But the sun-god remembered his promise and called to Gilgamesh out of the heavens, bidding him go forth unafraid to the combat. And even as the leaves of the thicket parted and the terrible face bore down upon the heroes, the sun-god sent mighty, searing winds from every quarter of the heavens, and they beat against the eye of the monster until they blinded his vision and he could move neither backward nor forward.

Then, as he stood there, thrashing with his arms, Gilgamesh and Enkidu closed in upon him, until at last he begged for grace. But the heroes would grant him none. They drew their swords and severed the horrible head from his giant frame.

Then Gilgamesh wiped the dust of battle from his brow and shook out the braid of his hair and removed his soiled garments and put on his kingly robe and crown. So wondrous did he appear in his beauty and valor that even a goddess could not resist him, and presently the Lady Ishtar herself was there at his side.

"Gilgamesh," said she, "come, be my lover. I will give you a chariot of gold encrusted with gems, and the mules that draw it shall be swift as the wind. You shall enter our house beneath the fragrance of cedars. Threshold and stoop shall kiss your feet. Kings and princes shall bow before you and bring you the yield of the earth for tribute. Your ewes shall bear twins; your chariot horses shall be chargers; and your oxen shall have no equal."

But Gilgamesh remained unmoved. "Lady," he replied, "you speak of giving me riches, but you would demand far more in return. The food and clothing you would need would be such as befits a goddess; the house would have to be meet for a queen, and your robes of the finest weave. And why should I give you all this? You are but a draughty door, a palace tottering to its ruin, a turban which fails to cover the head, pitch that defiles the hand, a bottle that leaks, a shoe that pinches.

"Have you ever kept faith with a lover? Have you ever been true to your troth? When you were a girl there was Tammuz. But what happened to him? Year by year men mourn his fate! He who comes to you preened like a jaybird ends with broken wings! He who comes like a lion, perfect in strength, you ensnare into pits sevenfold! He who comes like a charger, glorious in battle, you drive for miles with spur and lash, and then give him muddied water to drink! He who comes like a shepherd tending his flock you turn to a ravening wolf, scourged by his own companions and bitten by his own dogs!

"Remember your father's gardener? What happened to *him?* Daily he brought you baskets of fruit, daily bedecked your table. But when he refused your love you trapped him like a spider caught in a spot where it cannot move! You will surely do the same to me."

When Ishtar heard these words she was very angry, and rushed to her father and mother in heaven to complain of the insults which the hero had hurled at her. But the heavenly father refused to interfere, and told her roundly that she had got what she deserved.

Then Ishtar fell to threats. "Father," she cried, "I want

you to send against this fellow that mighty heavenly bull whose rampaging brings storms and earthquakes. If you refuse I will break down the doors of hell and release the dead, so that they arise and outnumber the living!"

"Very well," said her father at length, "but remember, whenever the bull comes down from heaven it means a seven-year famine on earth. Have you provided for that? Have you laid up food for men and fodder for beasts?"

"I have thought of all that," replied the goddess. "There is food enough for men and fodder for beasts."

So the bull was sent down from heaven and straightway rushed upon the heroes. But even as it charged, snorting and foaming in their faces, flaying and thrashing with its mighty tail, Enkidu seized its horns and thrust his sword into the back of its neck. Then they plucked out its heart and brought it as an offering to the sun-god.

Meanwhile Ishtar was pacing up and down upon the ramparts of Erech, watching the fight in the valley below. When she saw that the bull had been vanquished she leaped upon the battlements and let out a piercing shriek.

"Woe betide Gilgamesh," she screamed, "who has dared to hold me in contempt and to slay the bull of heaven!"

At these words Enkidu, wishing to make it clear to her that he too had played his part in the victory, tore off the buttocks of the bull and flung them in her face.

"Would that I could lay hands on *you*," he cried, "and do the same to you! Would that I could tear out your entrails and hang them up beside this bull's!"

Ishtar was now thoroughly put out, and all that she could do was to prepare to give decent burial to the bull, as befitted a heavenly creature. But even this was denied her, for the two heroes promptly picked up the carcass and carried it in triumph into Erech. So the goddess was left with her maidens, absurdly shedding tears over the animal's buttocks, while Gilgamesh and his comrade went striding merrily into the city, proudly displaying the evidence of their prowess and receiving the plaudits of the people.

But the gods are not mocked; whatsoever a man sows, that shall he also reap.

One night Enkidu had a strange dream. He dreamed that the gods were sitting in council, trying to decide whether he or Gilgamesh was the more to blame for the slaying of Humbaba and the heavenly bull. The more guilty, they had ruled, was to be put to death.

For a long while the debate raged back and forth, but when at length they had still not made up their minds, Anu, the father of the gods, proposed a way out.

"In my opinion," he declared, "Gilgamesh is the greater culprit, for not only did he slay the monster but he also cut down the sacred cedar."

No sooner, however, had he uttered these words than pandemonium broke loose, and soon the gods were at sixes and sevens, each roundly abusing the other.

"Gilgamesh?" screamed the god of the winds. "It is Enkidu who is the real villain, for it was he that led the way!"

"Indeed!" roared the sun-god, wheeling sharply upon him. "What right have *you* to talk? It was *you* who hurled the winds into Humbaba's face!"

"And what about *you?*" retorted the other, shaking with anger. "What about *you?* If it hadn't been for you, neither of them would have done these things! It was *you* that encouraged them and kept coming to their aid!"

Fiercely they argued and fiercely they wrangled, their tempers growing hotter by the minute and their voices louder and louder. But before they could come to a decision—Enkidu woke up.

He was now firmly convinced that he was doomed to die. But when he told the dream to his companion it seemed to Gilgamesh that the real punishment was destined, after all, for himself.

"Dear comrade," he cried, the tears streaming down his cheeks, "do the gods imagine that by killing you they will be letting me go free? Nay, good friend, all my days I shall sit like a beggar on the threshold of death, waiting for the door to open that I may enter and see your face!"

For the rest of the night Enkidu lay awake on his bed, tossing and turning. And as he lay, his whole life seemed to pass before him. He remembered the carefree days of old, when he had roamed the hills with the beasts, and then he bethought him of the huntsman who had found him and of the girl who had lured him to the world of men. He recalled also the adventure in the forest of cedars, and how the door had slammed shut on his hands, inflicting upon him the first and only wound that he had ever suffered. And he cursed the huntsman and the girl and the door with a bitter curse.

At last the first rays of the morning sun came stealing through the window, bathing the room in light and playing against the shadows on the opposite wall. "Enkidu," they seemed to be saying, "not all of your life among men has been darkness, and those whom you are cursing were rays of light. Were it not for the huntsman and the girl, you would still be eating grass and sleeping in cold meadows, but now you feed on the fare of kings and lie on a princely couch. And were it not for them, you would never have met with Gilgamesh, nor found the closest friend of your life!"

Then Enkidu knew that the sun-god had been speaking to him, and he no longer cursed the huntsman and the girl, but called down upon them all manner of blessings.

A few nights later he dreamed a second dream. This time it seemed as though a loud cry went up from heaven and earth, and a strange, grisly creature, with the face of a lion and the wings and talons of an eagle, swooped down from nowhere and carried him off. All of a sudden his arms sprouted feathers, and he became like the monstrous being which had assailed him. Then he knew that he was dead and that one of the harpies of hell was speeding him along the road of no return. At last he reached the house of darkness, where dwelt the shades of the departed. And behold, all the great ones of the earth were around him. Kings and nobles and priests, their crowns and robes put aside forever, sat huddled like hideous demons, covered with birdlike wings; and instead of the roasts and bakemeats of old they now ate dirt and dust. And there, on a lofty throne, sat the queen of hell herself, with her faithful handmaid squatting beside her, reading from a tablet the record of every soul as it passed in the gloom.

When he awoke Enkidu related the dream to his companion; and now they knew for certain which of them was doomed to die.

For nine days Enkidu languished upon his bed, growing weaker and weaker, while Gilgamesh watched beside him, torn with grief.

"Enkidu," he cried in his anguish, "you were the ax at my side, the bow in my hand, the dirk in my belt, my shield, my robe, my chiefest delight! With you I braved and endured all things, scaled the hills and hunted the leopard! With you I seized the heavenly bull and came to grips with the ogre of the forest! But now, behold, you are wrapped in sleep and shrouded in darkness, and hear not my voice!"

And even as he cried he saw that his companion no longer stirred nor opened his eyes; and when he felt Enkidu's heart it was beating no more.

Then Gilgamesh took a cloth and veiled the face of Enkidu, even as men veil a bride on the day of her espousal. And he paced to and fro and cried aloud, and his voice was the voice of a lioness robbed of her whelps. And he stripped off his garments and tore his hair and gave himself up to mourning.

All night long he gazed upon the prostrate form of his companion and saw him grow stiff and wizened, and all the beauty was departed from him. "Now," said Gilgamesh, "I have seen the face of death and am sore afraid. One day I too shall be like Enkidu."

When morning came he had made a bold resolve.

On an island at the far ends of the earth, so rumor had it, lived the only mortal in the world who had ever escaped death—an old, old man, whose name was Utnapishtim. Gilgamesh decided to seek him out and to learn from him the secret of eternal life.

As soon as the sun was up he set out on his journey, and at last, after traveling long and far, he came to the end of the world and saw before him a huge mountain whose twin peaks touched the sky and whose roots reached down to nethermost hell. In front of the mountain there was a massive gate, and the gate was guarded by fearsome and terrible creatures, half man and half scorpion.

Gilgamesh flinched for a moment and screened his eyes from their hideous gaze. Then he recovered himself and strode boldly to meet them.

When the monsters saw that he was unafraid, and when they looked on the beauty of his body, they knew at once that no ordinary mortal was before them. Nevertheless they challenged his passage and asked the purpose of his coming.

Gilgamesh told them that he was on his way to Utnapishtim, to learn the secret of eternal life.

"That," replied their captain, "is a thing which none has ever learned, nor was there ever a mortal who succeeded in reaching that ageless sage. For the path which we guard is the path of the sun, a gloomy tunnel twelve leagues long, a road where the foot of man may not tread."

"Be it never so long," rejoined the hero, "and never so dark, be the pains and the perils never so great, be the heat never so searing and the cold never so sharp, I am resolved to tread it!"

At the sound of these words the sentinels knew for certain that one who was more than a mortal was standing before them, and at once they threw open the gate.

Boldly and fearlessly Gilgamesh entered the tunnel, but with every step he took the path became darker and darker, until at last he could see neither before nor behind. Yet still he strode forward, and just when it seemed that the road would never end, a gust of wind fanned his face and a thin streak of light pierced the gloom.

When he came out into the sunlight a wondrous sight met

his eyes, for he found himself in the midst of a faery garden, the trees of which were hung with jewels. And even as he stood rapt in wonder the voice of the sun-god came to him from heaven.

"Gilgamesh," it said, "go no farther. This is the garden of delights. Stay awhile and enjoy it. Never before have the gods granted such a boon to a mortal, and for more you must not hope. The eternal life which you seek you will never find."

But even these words could not divert the hero from his course and, leaving the earthly paradise behind him, he proceeded on his way.

Presently, footsore and weary, he saw before him a large house which had all the appearance of being a hospice. Trudging slowly toward it, he sought admission.

But the alewife, whose name was Siduri, had seen his approach from afar and, judging by his grimy appearance that he was simply a tramp, she had ordered the postern barred in his face.

Gilgamesh was at first outraged and threatened to break down the door, but when the lady called from the window and explained to him the cause of her alarm his anger cooled, and he reassured her, telling her who he was and the nature of his journey and the reason he was so disheveled. Thereupon she raised the latch and bade him welcome.

Later in the evening they fell to talking, and the alewife attempted to dissuade him from his quest. "Gilgamesh," she said, "that which you seek you will never find. For when the gods created man they gave him death for his portion; life they kept for themselves. Therefore enjoy your lot. Eat, drink, and be merry; for *that* were you born!"

But still the hero would not be swerved, and at once he

proceeded to inquire of the alewife the way to Utnapishtim.

"He lives," she replied, "on a faraway isle, and to reach it you must cross an ocean. But the ocean is the ocean of death, and no man living has sailed it. Howbeit, there is at present in this hospice a man named Urshanabi. He is the boatman of that aged sage, and he has come hither on an errand. Maybe you can persuade him to ferry you across."

So the alewife presented Gilgamesh to the boatman, and he agreed to ferry him across.

"But there is one condition," he said. "You must never allow your hands to touch the waters of death, and when once your pole has been dipped in them you must straightway discard it and use another, lest any of the drops fall upon your fingers. Therefore take your ax and hew down six-score poles; for it is a long voyage, and you will need them all."

Gilgamesh did as he was bidden, and in a short while they had boarded the boat and put out to sea.

But after they had sailed a number of days the poles gave out, and they had well nigh drifted and foundered, had not Gilgamesh torn off his shirt and held it aloft for a sail.

Meanwhile, there was Utnapishtim, sitting on the shore of the island, looking out upon the main, when suddenly his eyes descried the familiar craft bobbing precariously on the waters.

"Something is amiss," he murmured. "The gear seems to have been broken."

And as the ship drew closer he saw the bizarre figure of Gilgamesh holding up his shirt against the breeze.

"That is not my boatman," he muttered. "Something is surely amiss."

When they touched land Urshanabi at once brought his passenger into the presence of Utnapishtim, and Gilgamesh told him why he had come and what he sought.

"Young man," said the sage, "that which you seek you will never find. For there is nothing eternal on earth. When men draw up a contract they set a term. What they acquire today, tomorrow they must leave to others. Age-long feuds in time die out. Rivers which rise and swell, in the end subside. When the butterfly leaves the cocoon it lives but a day. Times and seasons are appointed for all."

"True," replied the hero. "But you yourself are a mortal, no whit different from me; yet you live forever. Tell me how you found the secret of life, to make yourself like the gods."

A faraway look came into the eyes of the old man. It seemed as though all the days of all the years were passing in procession before him. Then, after a long pause, he lifted his head and smiled.

"Gilgamesh," he said slowly, "I will tell you the secret— a secret high and holy, which no one knows save the gods and myself." And he told him the story of the great flood which the gods had sent upon the earth in the days of old, and how Ea, the kindly lord of wisdom, had sent him warning of it in the whistle of the wind which soughed through the wattles of his hut. At Ea's command he had built an ark, and sealed it with pitch and asphalt, and loaded his kin and his cattle within it, and sailed for seven days and seven nights while the waters rose and the storms raged and the lightnings flashed. And on the seventh day the ark had grounded on a mountain at the end of the world, and he had opened a window in the ark and sent out a dove, to see if the waters had subsided. But the dove had returned, for want of place to rest. Then he had sent out a swallow, and the swallow too had come back. And at last he had sent out a raven, and the raven had not returned. Then he had led forth his kinsmen and his cattle and offered thanksgiving to the gods. But suddenly the god of the winds had come down from heaven and led him back into the ark, along with his wife, and set it afloat upon the waters once more, until it came to the island on the far horizon, and there the gods had set him to dwell forever.

When Gilgamesh heard the tale he knew at once that his quest had been vain, for now it was clear that the old man had no secret formula to give him. He had become immortal, as he now revealed, by special grace of the gods and not, as Gilgamesh had imagined, by possession of some hidden knowledge. The sun-god had been right, and the scorpion-men had been right, and the alewife had been right: that which he had sought he would never find—at least on this side of the grave.

When the old man had finished his story he looked steadily into the drawn face and tired eyes of the hero. "Gilgamesh," he said kindly, "you must rest awhile. Lie down and sleep for six days and seven nights." And no sooner had he said these words than, lo and behold, Gilgamesh was fast asleep.

Then Utnapishtim turned to his wife. "You see," said he, "this man who seeks to live forever cannot even go without sleep. When he awakes he will, of course, deny it—men were liars ever—so I want you to give him proof. Every day that he sleeps bake a loaf of bread and place it beside him. Day by day those loaves will grow staler and moldier, and after seven nights, as they lie in a row beside him, he will be able to see from the state of each how long he has slept."

So every morning Utnapishtim's wife baked a loaf, and she made a mark on the wall to show that another day had passed; and naturally, at the end of six days, the first loaf was dried out, and the second was like leather, and the third was soggy, and the fourth had white specks on it, and the fifth was filled with mold, and only the sixth looked fresh.

When Gilgamesh awoke, sure enough, he tried to pretend that he had never slept. "Why," said he to Utnapishtim, "the moment I take a nap you go jogging my elbow and waking me up!" But Utnapishtim showed him the loaves, and then Gilgamesh knew that he had indeed been sleeping for six days and seven nights.

Thereupon Utnapishtim ordered him to wash and cleanse himself and make ready for the journey home. But even as the hero stepped into his boat to depart Utnapishtim's wife drew near.

"Utnapishtim," said she, "you cannot send him away empty-handed. He has journeyed hither with great effort and pain, and you must give him a parting gift."

The old man raised his eyes and gazed earnestly at the hero. "Gilgamesh," he said, "I will tell you a secret. In the depths of the sea lies a plant. It looks like a buckthorn and pricks like a rose. If any man come into possession of it, he can, by tasting it, regain his youth!"

When Gilgamesh heard these words he tied heavy stones to his feet and let himself down into the depths of the sea; and there, on the bed of the ocean, he espied the plant. Caring little that it pricked him, he grasped it between his fingers, cut the stones from his feet, and waited for the tide to wash him ashore.

Then he showed the plant to Urshanabi the boatman.

"Look," he cried, "it's the famous plant called Graybeard-grow-young! Whoever tastes it, gets a new lease on life! I will carry it back to Erech and give it to the people to eat. So will I at least have some reward for my pains!"

After they had crossed the perilous waters and reached land, Gilgamesh and his companion began the long journey on foot to the city of Erech. When they had traveled fifty leagues the sun was already beginning to set, and they looked for a place to pass the night. Suddenly they came upon a cool spring.

"Here let us rest," said the hero, "and I will go bathe."

So he stripped off his clothes and placed the plant on the ground and went to bathe in the cool spring. But as soon as his back was turned a serpent came out of the waters and, sniffing the fragrance of the plant, carried it away. And no sooner had it tasted of it than at once it sloughed off its skin and regained its youth.

When Gilgamesh saw that the precious plant had now passed from his hands forever he sat down and wept. But soon he stood up and, resigned at last to the fate of all mankind, he returned to the city of Erech, back to the land whence he had come.

Comment

The epic of Gilgamesh is, beyond doubt, the greatest literary masterpiece that has come down to us from the ancient Near East. Its popularity in ancient times is attested by the fact that, besides the main "edition" prepared for the library of King Ashurbanipal (669–628 B.C.) and now in the British Museum, we possess—albeit in fragmentary form—an older Assyrian, a Hittite, and even a Hurrian (Horite) version; while there is a whole cycle of earlier Sumerian legends dealing with the hero, and scenes from the epic may be recognized on cylinder seals dating back to the third millennium B.C. The epic was, in fact, the Iliad or Odyssey of the ancient Near East, and phrases from it are often affected by later writers, in much the same way that a modern English author might work in an expression from the Bible or Shakespeare.

Nevertheless, although it now presents a unified and consistent story, the epic is really a compilation of what were originally separate and independent tales, and it is probable that these tales, like those of the *Iliad* and *Odyssey,* had long been known from oral transmission before the master hand of a great poet grouped them around a central character of tradition and thereby welded them into a whole. Many of them have extensive parallels in other cultures.

Take, for example, the initial meeting between the hero Gilgamesh and his companion, Enkidu. The encounter between the great domesticated hero and a wild and woolly vagabond is the theme of countless stories among all peoples, as, for instance, that of Jacob and Esau in the Bible or of Proetus and Acrisius in Greek myth; while the picture of the semi-human man covered with hair (F 521.1), consorting with animals (F 567), and eventually tamed by a woman (D 733.1) is likewise not unknown. But what is here of special interest is that the meeting takes place at the New Year festival. Gilgamesh, as king of Erech, is about to celebrate the traditional rite of the "sacred marriage" when Enkidu rudely bars his path and flings down a challenge. Then they fall to and engage in combat. Now the fact is that the part played by Enkidu is precisely that of the so-called Impostor (or Interloper) in popular literature and drama from several parts of the world. In Thrace and Northern Greece, for instance, it is customary to perform a rude pantomime on certain crucial calendar dates, and an essential element of the plot is that a black-masked, uncouth braggart breaks in upon a wedding feast, attempts to molest the bride, and engages in combat with the bridegroom. In Thessaly he is usually regarded as a wild and woolly "Arab" and, to indicate his barbarous character, he wears a black mask of sheep- or goatskin, a sheepskin coat, and sometimes even a tail. Elsewhere in the same general area the two antagonists are known as "bridegroom" and "Arab." [1]

The Impostor is also frequently a character in European folktales. The late Edwin S. Hartland, in his famous book, *The Legend of Perseus*,[2] has collected no less than twenty-five instances of his appearance, and has called attention to the significant fact that he is often portrayed as a Negro. Similarly, the late Francis Cornford has observed a survival of this character in the familiar figure of the intruder or interloper who interrupts the scenes of feasting or marriage in the comedies of Aristophanes.[3]

In the light of these parallels, it is not unreasonable to suppose that the incident of the encounter between Gilgamesh and Enkidu derives from what was originally an independent story dealing with an imaginary interruption of the traditional New Year rites by an impudent and uncouth upstart.

Take, again, the adventure of the two heroes against Humbaba, the dread ogre of the forest of cedars. This falls into a pattern familiar in the popular lore of the entire world. The ogre lives on the top of a mountain (F 531.6.2.1). His shouts are storms (F 531.3.8), and he breathes fire (B 14.1). Also he evidently possessed a gorgon-like face which had the ability to petrify all

---

[1] A. J. B. Wace, "North Greek Festivals," in *Annual of the British School at Athens,* vol. xvi (1909–10), pp. 233 ff.

[2] London: D. Nutt, 1894–96.

[3] Francis M. Cornford, *The Origin of Attic Comedy* (London: E. Arnold, 1914), pp. 132–53.

on whom it gazed (D 581; F 526.3), for it is only when the winds blind his eye that he is defeated; and we happen to know that hideous gorgon-like masks were known in later times as "Humbaba heads." Lastly, he is said to wear seven cloaks. Humbaba is thus of a piece with the Libyan Gorgon Katoblepas, the Irish Balor, the Welsh Ispaddaden Pennkawr and the Serbian Vy, each of whom is a monstrous ogre who is said to ward off assailants by fixing his deadly eye upon them. Now, the curious thing is that in many of these cases the ogre is described expressly as screening his eye with seven veils when he is not using it for sinister purposes (D 2071.0.1). As a matter of fact, a modern Greek folk tale from the isle of Zacynthus offers an almost perfect analogue to the episode in the epic of Gilgamesh, for it relates how two heroes made the perilous ascent to the top of a mountain in order to attack a giant who possessed a deadly eye which he kept hidden under seven cloths.[4]

The conclusion is obvious: this incident in our story was once an independent tale. The seven cloaks of Humbaba are but a dim reminiscence of the characteristic seven veils.

Then there is the singular episode of the door. When Gilgamesh and his companion approach the forest of cedars, they first discover a door. Enkidu, it would appear, pushed it open or peers through a crack in it, for it is then that he reveals to Gilgamesh that Humbaba, who normally wears seven cloaks, is now clad in but one. Then he suddenly starts complaining that the door has injured his hand, a complaint which he later repeats when he lies on his deathbed and reviews his misfortunes.

As it stands, this episode remains without adequate explanation. It so happens, however, that there exists elsewhere a fairly widespread tale which relates how a mortal who had chanced upon the secret treasure trove or hideout of the gods or trolls,

---

[4] Arthur B. Cook, *Zeus: A Study in Ancient Religion* (London: Cambridge University Press, 1914–40), vol. ii (1924), p. 994.

neglected, on leaving the spot, to observe some divine injunction or taboo, whereupon the door swung automatically upon its hinges and injured his hand or foot (F 91.1). Here, for example, is a tale of this type from the Harz Mountains: [5]

The White Lady of Harzburg, a ghost suffering from a malediction, gives a flower to a charcoal-burner and leads him to a cavern in the mountain, directing him to fill his knapsack with treasures but not to open it before crossing water. He leaves the grotto, but forgets the flower, and the door closes behind him forever with such violence that it almost strikes off his heel. Had he taken the flower with him, he might have revisited the cavern many another time.

Similarly, in a story from Hessen, the peasant who forgets the magic flower finds that the door closes with such violence that it severs both his heels; while in a Bohemian version, he almost loses his hands. In Iceland the same thing is told of the priest Saemundur, who went to the devil's school to learn the black art. When he tried to cheat the devil of his fee by substituting his cloak for his person, the door automatically closed, injuring one of his heels.[6]

Jakob Grimm, in his *Deutsche Mythologie,* draws attention to the fact that in one version of the familiar German legend Brunhilde expresses the wish that she may follow Sigurd in death "lest the door fall upon his heel"; and he adds that this is "a formula often used on entering a closed cavern."

Once again the conclusion is obvious: the mysterious episode in our epic originated in a popular tale of the type described. Whether, in some earlier version, Enkidu actually violated a taboo, or whether this was so standard an element of popular lore that no specific explanation was considered necessary cannot, of course, now be determined.

[5] H. Prohle, *Sagen des Ober-Harzes* (1854), p. 4.
[6] Alexander H. Krappe, *Balor with the Evil Eye* (New York: Institut des études françaises, Columbia University, 1927), p. 109.

Following his defeat of the monster Humbaba, our hero is tempted by the goddess Ishtar, whom he rudely rebuffs. In the original text, when Gilgamesh rejects the goddess, he tells her that once she loved a lion, but she dug sevenfold pits for it; once she loved a stallion, but she brought it under lash and spur. It is commonly supposed that this refers to an actual transformation of her lovers into beasts, and the parallel of Circe, who turned her suitors to swine, immediately springs to mind. One may wonder, however, whether the language is not purely metaphorical, the idea being that, once the goddess lays hands on them, intrepid warriors are turned into drudges and brave heroes ruined. That is the interpretation which has here been adopted. It should be mentioned, however, that the magical transformation of lovers into animals is indeed attested elsewhere in popular literature (G 263.1), and that it is often a mere euphemism for death.

The bull of heaven is yet another character drawn from the storehouse of popular ideas. The idea is obvious enough: the noise of thunder suggests the roaring of a bull, and the bull is therefore everywhere the symbol of the storm-god.[7] Among the Hittites, Teshub was so conceived, and among the Babylonians, Ramman; while a Bushman tale regards rain as an ogre in bull form (G 372).

Enkidu's dream of the netherworld bears a marked resemblance to that of Kessi in the Hittite tale presented elsewhere in this volume (p. 144), and follows a fairly standardized pattern of the Vision of Hell. The messenger has eagle-like talons, in accordance with the ancient notion that giant birds escort the soul to the infernal regions. At Ischali have been found a number of terracotta plaques showing a heavily armed god encased in feathers and with talons for feet, and it has been suggested that this is a representation of Nergal, the Babylonian lord of the netherworld.

[7] L. Malten, *Der Stier in Kult und mythischer Bild* (1928); Mircea Eliade, *Traité d'histoire des réligions* (Paris: Payot, 1949), pp. 85 ff.

The souls of the dead were frequently regarded as taking the form of birds (E 732), and in Romanized Syria tombstones were often engraved with figures of birds. It is possible, indeed, that there is an allusion to this idea in the words of the Psalmist (90:10): "The days of our years are threescore years and ten, or even by reason of strength fourscore years; yet is their pride but labor and sorrow; for swiftly it passes, *and we fly away*"—literally, "take wing."

The journey through the subterranean tunnel is another episode of the epic which may well have originated as an entirely independent tale. The belief in such a tunnel is widespread (F 721.1), and among many peoples attempts have even been made to determine its location. A favorite notion is that it is to be identified with the rock tunnel, about eleven hundred meters in length, which extends from Bylkalein to the main source of the River Tigris. Hittite texts speak often of the "underground highway of the sun," and an Estonian tale relates how a prince once found himself in front of a secret door which opened upon the road to hell.[8] The entrance to the tunnel is usually placed in a mountain, since the sun is seen to set beneath the hills. In our present version this is called "the Mountain Mashu," but Mashu is a Babylonian word meaning "twin," so that what is indicated is the twin-peaked mythological mountain which is frequently depicted on early Babylonian cylinder seals. Certainly the name does *not* indicate Mons Masius, the modern Tur Abdin, in Armenia, as some have supposed.

On emerging from the tunnel, Gilgamesh comes upon the garden of delights, a kind of earthly paradise. This too is part of the stock-in-trade of popular lore (A 151.2; F 111). A garden of this kind, likewise situated on the top of the mountains, and actually styled an "Eden," is described in the twenty-eighth chapter of the Book of Ezekiel in the Bible, and it is significant that the inhabit-

[8] Hugo Gressmann and A. Ungnad, *Das Gilgamesch-Epos* (Göttingen: Vandenhoeck & Ruprecht, 1911), p. 162.

ant of it is there said to have been adorned with "every precious stone" and to have "walked up and down amid flashing gems," for this accords with the statement in our story that the trees of the garden bore jewels instead of fruit—a trait which recurs, incidentally, in folk descriptions of paradise (F 811.2.2).

Then comes the adventure with Siduri, the alewife. In the original version of the story Siduri was probably a Calypso-like figure who lived in the heart of the sea and guarded the tree of eternal life.[9] She was introduced as a character of legend, alternative to the ageless hero of the Flood, from whom Gilgamesh expected to learn the secret of immortality. By the time the tale reached its present form, however, she had lost much of her pristine character and had come to represent a somewhat different ideal. Far from being a mere seductive siren, Siduri is here the placid hostess of a wayside inn—a woman who has seen so much of God's creatures that she has achieved something of His infinite patience and serenity; a woman who is forever the hostess to strangers, each coming and going upon his own errand. The implication of the episode is that a man who has spurned even the faery garden of delights, where the trees are hung with jewels, might still, perhaps, find ease and contentment in the calm of a country inn.

If one looks for a modern analogue to Siduri, she is not hard to find. For her sisters are not only Calypso and Circe, but also the fat woman who kept the Potwell Inn in H. G. Wells' *Mr. Polly:*

The really pleasant thing in the spectacle . . . was quite the plumpest woman Mr. Polly had ever seen, seated in an arm-chair in the midst of all these bottles and glasses and glittering things, peacefully and tranquilly, and without the slightest loss of dignity, asleep. Many people would have called her a fat woman, but Mr. Polly's innate sense of epithet told him from the outset that plump was the word. She had

[9] See fully: W. F. Albright, "The Babylonian Sage Ut-napištim rûqu," in *Journal of the American Oriental Society,* vol. xxxviii (1918), pp. 60–65; "The Goddess of Life and Wisdom," in *American Journal of Semitic Languages,* vol. xxxvi (1920), pp. 258–94; M. Eliade, op. cit., pp. 248 ff.

shapely brows and a straight, well-shaped nose, kind lines and contentment about her mouth, and beneath it the jolly chins clustered like chubby little cherubim about the feet of an Assumption-ing Madonna. Her plumpness was firm and pink and wholesome, and her hands, dimpled at every joint, were clasped in front of her; she seemed, as it were, to embrace herself with infinite confidence and kindliness, as one who knew herself good in substance, good in essence, and would show her gratitude to God by that ready acceptance of all that He had given her. Her head was a little on one side, but just enough to speak of trustfulness and rob her of the stiff effect of self-reliance. And she slept.

"*My* sort," said Mr. Polly, and opened the door very softly.

Finally there is the voyage across the waters of death to the mystic isle where dwells the primeval sage Utnapishtim. The whole picture is painted along conventional lines, and again one is led to suspect that some traditional tale of the wondrous journey really underlies it. The theme recurs repeatedly in folk literature and is usually embellished with precisely the same details as are found in our story.

The island—a kind of Oriental Avalon—lies "at the confluence of the two streams." It is at the same spot that the dwelling of the gods is located in the Canaanite myths from Ras Shamra, and there is a curious passage in the Koran (*Sura* 18, 59 ff.) which speaks of "the junction of the two seas" as an especially wondrous place. What is meant is simply the horizon, where the waters which are above the earth meet those which are beneath it. The isle is thus the familiar Isle of the Blest, which lies where the sun sets (A 692). Around it flows the Perilous River. Although this is described as filled with "death-giving waters," it is *not* the river of death (A 672), the equivalent of the classical Styx, but rather the familiar mythical stream which separates the earth from the realm beyond it (F 141.1.1), i.e., the classical Okeanos. Similarly, Urshanabi is no Charon, as has been all too commonly supposed.

For what we have here is a journey not to the netherworld (F 80) but to a terrestrial otherworld (F 110) of the type especially familiar from the *imrama* tales of Irish folk literature. Characteristically enough, the hero is passed on from one person to another until he reaches his goal (H 1235)—a motif which is familiar to students of folklore under the catchname "Old, Older, Oldest," the underlying idea being that he moves by progressive stages back to the hoary Nestor who possesses the knowledge he seeks. But in the present case, the genius of the writer transcends his material: the quest is vain.

Finally, there has been considerable misunderstanding about the concluding episode of our story. The common view is that Utnapishtim tries to soften the disappointment of Gilgamesh by showing him how he can obtain a plant of immortality. But this is not, in fact, what the original text says, and such an interpretation destroys the whole point. The plant in question is *not* a plant of immortality but only the next best thing—one which rejuvenates the old and decrepit and thereby renders mortality just that much the more tolerable. The belief in such a plant is a commonplace of folklore in many parts of the world (D 1338.2). Analogously, the *haoma* of ancient Iranian mythology is sometimes represented as a plant which grows on an island in the lake of Vurakasha and the juice of which possesses the quality of removing decrepitude and renewing all things.[10] Moreover, just as it is here eaten by the serpent, so, in Iranian myth, the evil power Ahriman creates a lizard to feed on it.[11] Similarly, too, the *soma* of Indic belief is a kind of elixir of life contained in the juice of a paradisal plant.

[10] Videvdat xx, 4; Bundahisn xxvii, 4.
[11] Bundahisn I, i, 5.

2

THE WAR
OF THE GODS

Once upon a time there was no heaven and no earth. There was nothing in the world but water and the two great beings who ruled it. The fresh water belonged to Apsu, and the salt water to his wife, Tiamat. But at that time the two mixed and mingled together, for there were as yet neither rivers nor seas.

Out of their marriage there sprang at length two colossal creatures, Lahmu and his mate, Lahamu; and from them, in turn, rose a second pair, Anshar and his mate, Kishar. Anshar was the spirit of all above, and Kishar the spirit of all below; and from them came Anu, or Heaven.

The son of Anu was Ea, wise as he was strong, far superior to his parents and to any that had been before him.

After the birth of Ea, the family of the gods grew apace, and a loud and noisy crew they were! Up and down they raced, bawling and screaming at the tops of their voices, until poor Grandma Tiamat was nothing but a bundle of nerves. Nevertheless she suffered in silence and made no complaint. "Children are children," thought she, "and what cannot be cured must be endured." But Grandpa Apsu was of another mind, and one day he could stand the din no longer. So he sent for Mummu, the dwarf whom he kept in his house to counsel and amuse him.

"Come," said he, "let us go together to Tiamat and talk to her about it." And off they went to Tiamat to discuss what to do about the children.

But Apsu was in no mood for quiet discussion. "Listen," he cried, "I can stand it no more—not a moment's rest by day, and not a wink of sleep at night. We must have our peace and quiet, and I am going to get rid of them all!"

When she heard these words, Tiamat, pale with anger, turned to Apsu. "What do you mean?" she thundered. "Are we now to destroy what we ourselves created? Of course they set us on edge, as all children do older people, but we should take it in our stride!"

But her words had no effect. As soon as she had spoken them Mummu sidled up to his master and whispered in his ear. "Sir," said he, "take no notice. If you want your peace and quiet, go ahead and destroy them!"

The advice delighted Apsu. Lifting the dwarf upon his knees, he threw his arms around his neck and kissed him. Then they set off together to tell the gods what they had decided.

When the gods heard the decision they were seized with panic and started rushing to and fro across the vault of heaven, wringing their hands in wild dismay. Then they sat down in a gloomy, mournful silence, brooding on the fate that hung over their heads.

All except Ea, the wisest and shrewdest and most subtle of all the hosts of heaven, to whom there is nothing unforeseen, and nothing which he cannot forestall. While all his brothers and sisters huddled together in helpless despair,

Ea was busy forming a plan. Suddenly, without a word, he rose from his seat, took a pitcher and filled it with water, and recited over it a high and holy spell. Then he brought it to Apsu and Mummu and bade them drink.

Within a few moments Apsu was fast asleep, and Mummu was nodding his head, drowsy and scarcely able to keep awake. Ea lost no time. Quick as a flash, he ripped off Apsu's loincloth and crown and removed his halo and put them on himself. Then he bound Apsu in fetters and slew him and seized his dwelling. As for the wicked counselor Mummu, he trussed him up, passed a ring through his nose, and dragged him away to a dungeon.

When he had conquered his enemies and set up a pillar to record his triumph, he made a gay and beautiful bower, and when he had finished it he took Damkina, his bride. And there, in that holy and blessed abode, there was born to them the mightiest and strongest of gods, the prince of princes, the king of kings, LORD MARDUK HIMSELF. At the breasts of goddesses was he suckled, and along with their milk he drank majesty and power. Lithe was his figure, lustrous his eyes, lordly his gait; and he was fully mature from the day of his birth. No sooner did his father behold Marduk than he was filled with joy and his face shone, and he set on him the stamp of approval and decided then and there to confer on him a double meed of godhead. So Ea gave him a form so stately and grand that human mind cannot conceive it nor human tongue express it. Four eyes Marduk had, and four ears, and whenever his lips moved fire blazed forth from them. His stature was huge, and his limbs were immense, and he was clothed in the radiance of ten gods.

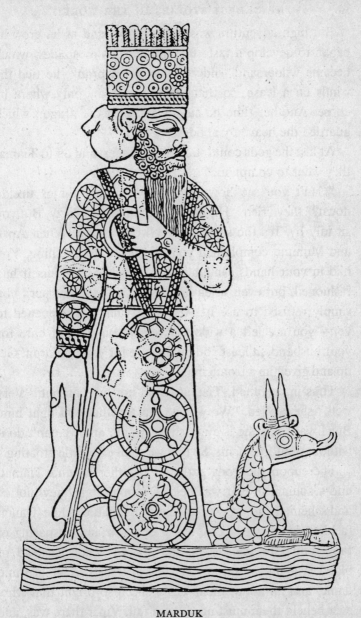

MARDUK

From a lapis lazuli cylinder seal, c. 850 B.C.

But high adventure was in his blood, and as he grew he began to develop a taste for mischievous escapades, which became wilder and wilder. Once, for a prank, he tied the winds on a leash, so that they could blow only where he chose. Another time he calmly muzzled the dragon which guarded the heavenly abodes.

At last the gods could stand it no longer, and off to Tiamat they went to complain.

"Can't you see how Marduk is turning things upside down?" they cried. "His antics are making us dizzy. But you sit idly by. It's the same story all over again. When Apsu and Mummu complained you refused to do anything. You had in your hands a mighty saw, which Apsu himself had fashioned, but even when he was in the deadliest peril you simply refused to use it! And look what has happened to you—you are left a widow. Even if you did not care for your husband, at least you might care for your children! Get up and give him a trouncing!"

Thus importuned, Tiamat could not but consent. "Very well," she replied. "We will go out together and fight him. But I warn you, he is a match for us all, and we can't do it without reinforcements. So first we shall do a little creating."

Thereupon the gods gathered together around Tiamat, and a council of war was held. Day and night they plotted and schemed and drew up plans for the battle, while Tiamat fashioned terrible beasts, sharp of tooth and unsparing of fang, and into their veins she poured venom instead of blood. Raging monsters they were, wreathed in fire and flame, and all about them was a sheen so bright that whoever beheld them must needs turn tail. Viper there was, and Dragon; Mammoth and Great Lion; Mad Dog and Scorpion-

Man; furious demons of the storm, Dragon-Fly and Cen-
taur—eleven horrible beings, fearless in combat, whose on-
slaught none could withstand.

Then she appointed, as commander of the host, a god
named Kingu. "Kingu," she said, "you shall raise the standard
and lead the charge and guard the spoil. Your word shall be
supreme, for, behold, I have raised you to high estate, and
you shall be as my consort!" And therewith she bestowed
upon him the symbols of power and fastened on his breast
the great Tablets of Decision. And when he had been in-
vested, Tiamat and Kingu together turned to the gods and
cried:

> "The fire may rage, the flame may burn;
>   Your breath shall put it out!
> The mightiest to a weakling turn,
>   The proud be put to rout!"

And with these words ringing in their ears the army set forth.

Meanwhile, Marduk himself knew nothing of what was
afoot. But as soon as Ea learned that his beloved son was
threatened he was filled with such anger and indignation
that he could not think clearly, but only sit and brood in
silence. At length, however, his hot-headedness gave way
to cool deliberation, and a plan came to his mind. At once
he rose up and went to Anshar. Shrewd and wise and subtle,
he knew full well how best to arouse that ancient god.

"Tiamat," said he, "is planning a rebellion against the
court of heaven." Then he told Anshar how Tiamat had
massed all the gods and created terrible monsters and was
already going forth to battle.

When Anshar heard these words he smote his thigh in

anger and bit his lip, and his heart was filled with foreboding. "Ea," cried he, "you have already shown your mettle by besting Apsu and Mummu. Now go forth again and slay Kingu and Tiamat!"

So Ea went forth to do battle against the advancing host, but when he saw the monsters marching in the van and the terrible sheen that enwrapped them, he was stricken with terror, turned tail, and fled.

When Anshar heard that Ea had been routed he was filled with dismay and summoned before him his son Anu.

"Anu," said he, "you are my firstborn, a hero whom none can withstand. Go now and confront Tiamat. Try first to soothe and appease her, but, if she will not listen, tell her that you come in my name and demand her obedience!"

Thereupon Anu departed and made straight for Tiamat. But when he beheld her furious mien and the terrible look upon her face, he too was stricken with terror and, like Ea, ran away.

Back he came to Anshar and reported what had happened. When Anu had finished speaking, Anshar turned to Ea and shook his head in despair; and all the hosts of heaven huddled together, muttering one to another, "Behold, there is none that can confront Tiamat and come back alive!"

There they sat, cowed, craven, and disconsolate, until at length Anshar rose from his throne and faced them in all his glory and might. "There is but one," he said, "who could ever be our champion—the stalwart warrior, the soldier intrepid, the valiant, impetuous Marduk himself!"

When Ea heard these words he summoned Marduk into an inner chamber so that he might speak privily with him. And he told him all about the plot of Tiamat. But he did not tell him that the plot was aimed against Marduk himself. "It is," he said, as he had told Anshar, "a rebellion against the court of heaven."

Then an earnest look stole across his face. "Marduk," he said slowly, "I am speaking to you now as your father, so listen carefully and obey. I want you to pay a visit to your great-grandfather Anshar. Though your brothers and sisters may complain about you, Anshar has always been partial to you, and he has a warm spot for you in his heart. When you come before him, strut around boldly, and wear your best soldierly expression, for that will especially amuse him."

So Marduk did as his father bade him, and paid a visit to Anshar and strutted before him like a man who is very sure of himself. And when Anshar saw his soldierly gait and bearing his heart was indeed cheered, and he kissed Marduk tenderly on the lips.

Marduk was deeply moved. "Anshar," he said softly, "you know that I have always loved you and that there is nothing which I would not do for your sake. My father has told me what is afoot, and how Tiamat is plotting a rebellion against the court of heaven. Who's afraid of that? Tiamat is only a woman, and I am ready to go out and fight her. In no time you will be trampling on her neck!"

"Very well," replied Anshar. "Go forth and confront her. See first if you can quiet her with words or some holy spell. But if she will not listen, mount the chariot of the whirlwind and fight!"

Marduk, however, was his father's son, and if he was strong and intrepid, he was also shrewd and ambitious. "This," thought he, "is my golden chance. Why should I brave the monsters and save the honor of heaven for nought?" So he squared his massive shoulders and looked his great-grandfather boldly in the face.

"Anshar," he said, "I am ready to go forth. But if I am to be your champion and conquer Tiamat and save your life, then you must make me chief of the gods. Go, call the assembly together and issue the decree! From now on, I alone shall make the decisions, and whatever I say shall be law!"

When he heard these words Anshar sent at once for his trusted messenger, Gaga.

"Go," said he, "to my aged parents Lahmu and Lahamu, whom you will find in the depths of the sea. Tell them that Tiamat is raising a rebellion against the court of heaven and that Marduk has offered to fight her on condition that he becomes chief of the gods. Explain to them that this is a decision which I cannot make alone, for it affects the hosts below no less than those above. So bid them gather together all the gods in their realm, and let them come hither that we may take counsel together!"

So Gaga went and delivered the message to Lahmu and Lahamu and told them all that had passed; and Lahmu and Lahamu in turn sent word to all the gods in their realm and bade them repair to the courts of heaven.

When the gods received the summons they could scarcely believe their ears. "Something unusual must have happened," they murmured, "for Tiamat to behave like this. We had better go and find out."

Presently the courts of heaven were thronged with gods and goddesses coming from all directions. As they met one another they would pause and embrace and exchange words of greeting. Then, when all were assembled, food and drink was set before them, and they sat down to a hearty banquet.

By the time the meeting came to order, all were in a happy and carefree mood, and as soon as the resolution was laid before them, no one bothered to challenge or contest it. A dais was hastily constructed, and Marduk was seated in triumph upon it, while the company showered upon him lavish expressions of praise and approval.

"Marduk for chieftain!" they cried. "Whatever he says shall be law! His to exalt, and his to abase! All the powers of Anu shall be conferred upon him! Marduk for king of the world, and may none of his arrows miss!"

Then someone brought forward a garment. "Marduk," they cried, "that you may show what power you have, say but the word and this garment shall be destroyed. Say but the word again, and it shall be whole!" *

So Marduk uttered the word, and, behold, the garment was destroyed. And again he uttered the word, and, behold, it was whole.

Then all the gods believed in Marduk, for they saw that his power was indeed supreme, and they bowed themselves low before him and cried out, "Marduk is king, Marduk is king!" And they handed him the scepter and set him upon the throne and placed in his hand the emblems of kingship, and they gave him a mighty sword and they said, "Go, cut the throat of Tiamat, and let the winds bear her blood away!"

As soon as the gods had returned to their homes, Marduk at once set about to prepare weapons for the combat. He took a bow in his hand and set an arrow within it, and before him he carried the flail of the lightning; and his whole body shone in the gleam. Then he made a net to imprison

* The word used in the original can also mean "vanish." Some scholars think, therefore, that Marduk made the garment vanish and then reappear.

his foes, and he created great stormwinds to march by his side.

When all was ready he grasped in his hand the great bludgeon of the thunder and mounted the chariot of the whirlwind. Four monsters were they that drew it: Rager, Ruthless, Stormer, and Fleet—each of them filled with venom, dauntless and sharp of tooth. Over his lips he smeared red ocher to protect him against the powers of evil; and in his hand was a fragrant herb to drown the stench of Tiamat and her beasts. Then he rode forth.

When Kingu and the vanguard saw him approaching they were filled with terror, for this they had not foreseen, and now all their plans were upset. But Tiamat herself neither wavered nor flinched. Boldly she strode forward, and the words of her war-song rent the air:

> "So you are the chief, you boast,
> And all must yield you place!
> Well, here come gods in a host,
> To challenge you face to face!"

No sooner, however, did the words reach his ears than Marduk raised his club and brandished it in her face and hurled back his retort:

> "Yours was the power and might,
> You were the queen of all;
> But nought to your heart was right
> Save quarrel and strife and brawl!
>
> You, whom we hailed as our mother,
> Have nought in your soul but spite;

Brother must strive with brother,
   And son against father must fight!

Brutal and base and black-hearted,
   Faithless to living and dead,
No sooner was Apsu departed
    Than Kingu you took in his stead!

What courage is this or defiance
   To challenge the ancient and old,
On monsters to place your reliance,
   To come forth with thousands untold?

Come forth by yourself, I say,
   Let your minions be banished from sight!
Come forth of yourself to the fray,
    And hand to hand let us fight!"

At these words Tiamat was stung to frenzy and, without looking to left or to right, she lunged blindly at her taunter, jaws agape to swallow him up; and even as she advanced, screaming insult and defiance, the gods who rode at her side furbished their weapons for combat.

But Marduk was too quick. No sooner did he see her bearing down upon him than, quick as a flash, he spread his net in her path and enmeshed her, and in less time than it takes to tell she was struggling furiously within it. Then he called to the stormwind, who had been marching in the rear of his host, and bade him advance. And the stormwind charged forward and rushed into the gaping jaws of Tiamat, so that she could not close her lips. Instantly Marduk drew his bow and shot his dart into the wide-open mouth, and the dart went down into Tiamat's maw and rent her veins and pierced her heart. Then, as her great body sagged and fell, he bound her and extinguished her life; and upon her prostrate corpse he planted his heel.

When the hosts of Tiamat saw that their leader had been slain, they broke ranks and attempted to flee, but at once the forces of Marduk closed in upon them and bound them in fetters and broke their weapons. And Marduk took them and placed them in a net and hurled them down into the caverns of the earth, to remain there as prisoners forever. The eleven monsters also he tied with ropes and trampled underfoot, so that all their might departed and all their pride was brought low, and they became as tame beasts upon a leash. As for Kingu, a special judgment was pronounced upon him: no more was he to be reckoned among the immortals.

Having thus disposed of her allies, Marduk turned again to the fallen Tiamat. Raising aloft his mighty club, he brought it down with full force upon her skull, and the wind bore away the blood from her severed veins.

When Anshar and Ea and all their companions saw what Marduk had done, they were overwhelmed with joy and relief, and at once they hastened toward him, bearing gifts and tribute. But Marduk would not stay to receive them, for already he was busy with other tasks; to him the end of Tiamat was but the beginning of his own new order. Taking the carcass of his prostrate foe, he split it in two like an oyster, and one half of it he raised aloft to form the firmament of heaven. Then he paced out the length of the waters which lay beneath that firmament, and he measured their width, and of the other half of Tiamat's body he made a kind of covering for them; and that covering was the foundation of the earth. And he set Anu in the realm that was above the firmament, and Enlil in the realm that was between the firmament and the earth, and Ea in the waters that were below the earth. So Anu became the god of the sky, and Enlil the god of the air, and Ea the god of the deep.

Then Marduk assigned places to all the other gods, and he created luminaries to shine in the heavens—even the sun and the moon and the stars—and he arranged the times and seasons of their movements. And he made courses for the stars, and he determined the lengths of the months; and he opened a gate in the east whence the sun might come forth at dawn, and a gate in the west whither it might repair at dusk.

But, behold, when all was set in order the gods came clustering around him, making bitter complaint. "Lord Marduk," they cried, "you have given us places and stations and assigned to each of us a task. But none have you appointed to serve us and sustain us while we perform them. Who is to tend our homes and give us our food?"

When Marduk heard these words he fell into deep thought. Then suddenly his face lit up. "I know what I will do," said he to himself. "I will take blood and bone and fashion a little puppet. Its name shall be Man. Man shall serve the gods and tend their needs while they perform their tasks!"

But when he imparted this plan to Ea, that wise and shrewd old god was able at once to improve upon it. "Why make new blood and bone?" he asked. "Let one of the rebels supply them!"

So Marduk ordered the bound rebels to be brought before him, and he questioned them closely and bade them declare in truth who was the prime offender of them all, that he might be put to death.

Now, the rebels had been simple soldiers in the host of Tiamat, and they saw no reason why any of them should bear the guilt of the war. "The prime offender," they replied with one accord, "was Kingu. He was our leader and commander, who both planned the attack and led it!"

Thereupon Kingu was led forth from his dungeon and delivered into the hands of Ea. And Ea cut off his head and slit open his veins, and out of the bone and blood he fashioned a puppet called Man, to serve the gods and tend their needs.

Then the gods gathered around Marduk in great joy. "Lord Marduk," they cried, "you have eased our burden and lightened our labors, and we would show you our thanks by building you a shrine on earth where you too may rest awhile from your toils. Year by year we will come to that shrine and pay you homage and sing your praise."

So for two whole years they worked and slaved with brick and mortar, and in the third year the city of Babylon was upreared, and towering above it was the palace of Esagila, the shrine of Marduk.

When the building was completed all the gods gathered together and held a feast within it, and Marduk sat among them and received their homage and declared the laws and the fates and the destinies of the whole world. And he took the great bow wherewith he had vanquished his foe, and he hung it in the heavens for all to see.

And so it remains unto this day. Man is the servant of the gods; and each New Year's Day the gods repair to the shrine of Marduk in Babylon to pay homage to him; and he declares to them the fates and destinies of the whole world. And the Bow hangs in heaven, for all to see.

Comment

"The War of the Gods" is more than a pure folktale. It was solemnly recited by the high priest in the innermost shrine of the temple on the fourth day of the Babylonian New Year festival, and it was, in a sense, the "book of words" of that occasion—a kind of primitive cantata.

In most cities of Babylonia the New Year festival, which lasted ten or eleven days, was celebrated at the beginning of spring; in some, at the beginning of autumn. The central theme of the festival was the renewal of life. This involved a re-establishment of the world order, a re-enthronement and confirmation of the king, and a determination by the gods of all human destinies for the coming twelve months. All of this was enacted in pantomime as part of the ceremonies, and that pantomime was thought, in turn, to represent what had likewise taken place at the beginning of time. The principal god was portrayed as doing battle with the demon forces of chaos and, after worsting them, establishing anew the order of creation. In token of his triumph, his image was formally paraded through the streets, to be finally installed in a special pavilion or shrine. All of the neighboring gods paid state visits for the occasion, and their statues too were carried along in the procession. Then the chief god, surrounded by his "visitors," held session in a special chamber, and the fates of men were decided. As a further element of the proceedings the king was formally deposed and then reinstated, to symbolize the fact that he personified a communal life which annually passed into eclipse and was subsequently renewed.

Ceremonies of this kind, involving mimetic combats with dragons (see p. 140), triumphal parades, and the formal deposition and reinstatement of the king, are common in many parts of the world. The curious reader need be referred only to the mass of examples collected by the late Sir James Frazer in his classic work, *The Golden Bough*. He may be reminded also that the kings and queens of the May, so familiar from folk custom—and even our own "beauty queens" and "Miss Rheingolds"—are but a dim survival of the annual re-enthronement of the sovereign.

Our principal version of "The War of the Gods" comes from the library of King Ashurbanipal (669–626 B.C.). The original tablets, unearthed in the nineteenth century, are now in the British Museum. But although these tablets were found at Nineveh, the later capital of Assyria, the version of the story which is inscribed upon them itself stems from Babylon and presents the form current in that city. The hero is therefore identified as Marduk, the principal god of the Babylonian metropolis, and the pavilion which is erected in his honor is Esagila, his great temple within it. In 1915, however, an older "edition" of the story, dating about 2000 B.C., was discovered at Asshur, the more ancient capital of Assyria, and there the hero is Asshur, the god of that country, and the pavilion is his famous temple in the Assyrian metropolis.

The story welds together into a seemingly consistent whole what may well have existed previously as a number of independent tales; and it is probable that "The War of the Gods" took a long time to develop into its present form. Throughout the narrative, a number of popular ideas are worked in and these ideas recur in the folklore of other peoples.

The first principle was water—a notion which is common

in primitive cosmogonies (A 810) and which would have appealed especially to the Babylonians, seeing that their earliest cities were, in fact, built on lagoons. The first beings were created in pairs (cf. A 116). The hero god (i.e., Marduk) was a precocious child, born virtually mature (T 585), like Heracles in Greek myth, Moses in later Jewish legend,[1] and Ullikummi in the Hittite story of "The Monster Made of Stone" (see p. 110). He had four eyes—a trait likewise ascribed to Kronos [2] and (occasionally) to Persephone [3] in Greek myth—and fire blazed from his lips (B 742). His enemy, Tiamat, was invulnerable by ordinary weapons (B 11.12.1) and was overcome only when the stormwind rushed into her mouth and inflated her belly. The hero protected himself by smearing red paste on his lips, a detail which is explained by the fact that red is frequently used by primitive peoples as a means of forfending demons (D 1293.1).[4] In Israel, for example, the ashes of a red heifer removed impurity (Numbers 19:2). Kaffir women smear themselves with red clay after childbirth; while among the Galellas and Tabelorese children are daubed with red ocher at initiation. Similarly, too, red thread is often prescribed in primitive magic for the symbolic "binding" of enemies, or of the powers of darkness.[5] The creation of man from the blood of a slain god likewise finds close parallels elsewhere (cf. A 1211.1); in Indic mythology he springs from the blood of Purusa, and in Greek myth from that of the discomfited Titans.

Lastly, Marduk's suspension of his victorious bow in heaven is echoed in the early Arab legend which relates that the storm-

---

[1] See L. Ginzberg, *The Legends of the Jews* (Philadelphia: The Jewish Publication Society of America, 1909–38), vol. ii, p. 264; vol. iii, p. 468.

[2] Arthur B. Cook, *Zeus: A Study in Ancient Religion* (London: Cambridge University Press, 1914–40), vol. ii (1924), p. 553.

[3] Ibid., p. 1029.

[4] See Eva Wunderlich, *Die Bedeutung der roten Farbe im Kultus der Griechen und Römer* (Giessen: A. Töpelmann, 1925); Fr. von Duhn, "Rot und Tot," in *Archiv für Religionswissenschaft*, vol. ix (1906), pp. 1–24.

[5] E.g., Theocritus, Idyll ii, 2; Petronius, *Satyricon*, 131.

god Qozah set up his triumphant bow in the sky after defeating the demon who caused the flood. In our story, it should be added, the bow in question is not the rainbow, as might be supposed, but a constellation (see pp. 187 ff.).

3

BORROWED PLUMES

Long, long ago, when the world was young, the eagle and the serpent were fast friends. When the eagle nested on the top of a tree, the serpent lay coiled at the bottom; and each watched over the other's young. Many a time the eagle would come flying from afar, bringing some tasty morsel for the baby snakes, and just as often the serpent would creep into the eagle's nest, carrying a choice tidbit for the eaglets.

One day when his brood had grown up the eagle began to think. "Now," thought he, "I don't need the serpent any longer. My children can fend for themselves. It's time I got something out of this for myself. Next time Master Serpent is away I'll swoop down and gobble up his young. And if I find anything else to eat—so much the better. I'll take it up aloft and have a nice little feast in the treetops!"

As he thought about it he grew more and more excited and began to talk aloud.

Now, among the eaglets there was one who was especially smart and clever, and no sooner did he overhear what his father was saying than he tried at once to dissuade him.

"Father!" he cried. "How can you think of such a thing? If you do it, it will bring you only sorrow. There is a god of justice in heaven, and he has a big net which covers the world. In it he catches everyone who disobeys his laws!"

But the eagle paid no attention to these words and, as soon as the serpent had left his home, down he swooped and carried off the young snakes.

When the serpent returned in the heat of the day, carrying his load of provisions and looking forward to his noontide nap, lo and behold, his home was a shambles, and his children were nowhere to be seen.

"Someone," said he, "has tried to attack them, and they have done what I always taught them to do."

Thereupon he started to dig, thinking that they must be hiding underground. But the deeper he dug and the higher the dust rose, the lower his spirits sank. At last the terrible truth dawned upon him. Away he sped, writhing and rattling and creeping and crawling, until he came into the presence of the god of justice himself.

"Sire," he cried, amid his tears, "Master Eagle and I had a bond of friendship, which we swore by your high and holy name. I, for my part, have kept good faith, but behind my back Master Eagle has raided my hole and gobbled up my young. While he sits proud and secure in his treetop, I go writhing in grief, robbed of my family, robbed of my home! I implore you to catch him in your net, that mighty, wide-flung net from which the guilty can never escape!"

When the god of justice heard these words he was moved to pity. "Master Serpent," he replied gently, gazing on the hapless, dust-stained creature before him, "take to the road and cross the hills. There, in a field beyond, you will find a buffalo lying on the ground. I have trapped it and felled it especially for you. Worm your way into its carcass and

THE FIGHT BETWEEN THE EAGLE AND THE SERPENT

Bas-relief from Nippur, twenty-fourth century B.C.

snuggle up inside. In a little while all the fowl of the air will come swooping upon it, and among them will come Master Eagle. He will have no idea that you are inside and will start flittering and fluttering and pecking and poking to get at the choicest parts of the meat. As soon as he reaches you, grab his wings and talons and tear them. Then, when he is utterly helpless, toss him into a ditch and let him lie there till he dies of hunger and thirst!"

So the serpent did as he was bidden and took to the road and crossed the hills and came upon the buffalo lying in a field and wormed his way into its carcass and snuggled up inside. In a little while all the fowl of the air came swooping upon it, to devour the flesh; and when the eagle saw what was happening he too called together his brood and made ready to descend.

Once again the smart and clever little eaglet tried to dissuade him. "Father," he cried, "stay where you are! Maybe there is a serpent lurking in that carcass!"

But again the eagle paid no attention to the words, and down he swooped, flittering and fluttering and pecking and poking to get at the choicest parts of the meat. Deeper and deeper he pecked and poked, until all of a sudden out popped the serpent and grabbed his wing.

"Let me go!" screamed the eagle in anguish. "Spare my life, and I will give you anything you ask. Spare me, and I will shower you with presents like a bride!"

But the serpent would not let go. "Never, never!" he cried. "For if I spared you the god of justice would hold me to account, and what answer could I give him? He would simply turn upon *me* the fate he has decreed for *you!*"

And therewith he tore the eagle's wings and talons, and

tossed him helpless into a ditch, to lie there and perish of hunger and thirst.

Meanwhile, in the great city of Kish, strange things were happening. The gods had taken a dislike toward the people who lived there and had met in council and decided to destroy them without issue.

For some time all the powers of heaven and earth had been marching around the city walls like an army of invaders, while seven mighty demons had kept the gates bolted and barred, so that no one might escape. Within the city plague and pestilence had been raging apace. Now at last they had claimed as victims not only the king but also all of his heirs, so that the people were left without leader or guide. To add to the city's plight, the gods had steadily refused to allow a successor to be appointed. All the emblems of kingship— the crown, the scepter, and the robes—which they were wont to bestow afresh upon each new monarch in token of their blessing and approval, were now kept locked and hidden in heaven. It was, indeed, as in those far-off days of old, when there were neither kings nor counselors on earth, and when the kingdom was the Lord's.

Yet, amid all the host of unfriendly gods, there were two who looked upon men with a more kindly eye. Up and down through the courts of heaven paced mighty Enlil, the god who installs sovereigns, searching, searching, searching for someone whom he might persuade to give succor; while down upon earth, through the highways and byways of the city, and even far into the fields beyond, roamed Mother Ishtar—she at whose breasts all kings are suckled—peering into the faces of men, seeking the one whom, even in defiance of the gods, she might call to the deliverance of the people.

At length, after both had searched for many days, their choice fell upon a humble shepherd, whose name was Etana.

"Yon Etana," they said, "is a good and faithful shepherd. He shall be king and shepherd the people."

So Etana was taken to the palace, and all the ceremonies of enthronement were performed. Priests and sorcerers besought the gods in prayer and set before them sumptuous viands and plenteous drink, that they might turn from their displeasure and bestow their grace upon monarch and realm. Then, as was the wont of that place, they led Etana into an inner chamber to be joined in marriage to a certain high and holy bride, so that, by the power and fruit of their espousals, the land and the people might have increase. But no matter how sumptuous the viands and how plenteous the drink, the gods were unwilling to stay their hands. The plague and pestilence raged unabated, and Etana's bride did not conceive.

At last, when he saw that the marriage remained without issue and that his people were now but a handful in number, he betook himself to the shrine of the god of justice and craved a boon.

"Sire," said he, as the tears ran down his cheeks, "no offering is there which my priests have not offered, no sacrifice which they have not presented. Yet, behold, our people die like flies, and no children are born unto us. Decree a halt to our sorrow, an end to our woe! Place in my hands the plant which causes birth by magic, so that I and my people may have increase, and this burden be lifted from us!"

Now, it so happened that while Etana was praying to the god of justice, so too was the eagle who had been left lying in the ditch. "Sire," said he, "if you will spare my life I will spend all the rest of my days reciting your praise!"

The god of justice answered both his suppliants.

To Etana he said, "Take to the road, cross the hills, and you will come to a ditch. Peer within, and you will see an eagle. That eagle will tell you where to find the magic plant."

And to the eagle he said, "You have done a vile and abominable thing. You are tainted and defiled. I cannot come near you. But I will send a mortal, and he will deliver you."

So there lay the eagle in the ditch, sighing and sobbing, when who should come along the road but Etana. As he reached the edge of the ditch he peered within, and, sure enough, there lay the eagle, helpless and unable to move.

"Hello," said the eagle feebly. "What brings you hither?"

But Etana was too amazed to reply. Now he knew that what the god had foretold had indeed come to pass.

"Friend," he stammered, "give me—show me—the plant which causes birth by magic!"

Then he collected himself. "But tell me," he added, "how is it that you are lying in this ditch in such a miserable state?"

"Ah," replied the eagle, "that is a long story. You must know that I am the king of the birds and can fly higher than any other. Well, one day quite recently I was flying blissfully along, minding my own business, when suddenly I found myself right in front of the courts of heaven. I passed through the first gate without trouble, and on through the second and the third and the fourth and the fifth and the sixth. But the moment I entered the seventh, which leads to the throne of Queen Ishtar, the lions which crouch at her feet sprang up with a roar and rushed at me. There was a tussle, of course, and that's how my wing got torn."

Then he lowered his voice. "For all that," he added, "I *did* catch a glimpse of something important: *the magic plant which you are seeking is up in that very court.* If you will mend my wing and lift me out of this ditch, I will gladly carry you there."

Etana was now beside himself with excitement and, although it took some effort, he managed at last to haul the eagle up from the ditch and repair his broken wing.

"Now," said the eagle, "we are ready. Place your chest against my back, hold on to my wings with your hands, and dig your elbows into my sides. I am about to take to the air."

Etana did as he was bidden, and through the heavens they flew, higher and ever higher. When they were a full league aloft the eagle turned his head and addressed his companion. "Friend," said he, "take a glance at the earth. Do you see the great mountain in the middle, and the ocean all around it?"

"All I see," replied Etana, "is a little mound and a tiny trickle of water."

Then they flew higher—a further league. Again the eagle turned his head. "How does the earth look now?" he asked.

"All I see," replied Etana, "is a small vegetable patch and beside it a puddle."

Yet another league they flew, and again the eagle turned his head. "And now?" he asked.

"Now," replied Etana, "I see nothing. I—I—" And suddenly his hands grew limp and his body slack, and he felt himself slipping—slipping . . .

ETANA FLYING TO HEAVEN

From a cylinder seal formerly in the collection of Lord Southesk

One league, two leagues, three leagues, he hurtled and plunged, and then there was a roar as of raging billows, and the ocean seemed to be coming to meet him.

Here ends the narrative on the clay tablet.

Then, in a moment, there was stillness, broken only by the plash of the waves and by the frightened cries of an eagle wheeling in dismay. But even as the waves swelled and broke they seemed to be repeating, over and over again, the words of a strange message:

> *Borrowed plumes are weak for flying:*
> *God's decrees are past defying.*

Comment

"Borrowed Plumes," or "The Man Who Flew to Heaven," is really two stories deftly rolled into one.

The first story revolves around the enmity of the eagle and the serpent. This was a piece of traditional animal lore,[1] based on the belief that each claimed to be deathless and regularly to renew its youth—the eagle by molting its feathers, and the serpent by sloughing its skin.

The constant rejuvenation of the eagle (B 758) is mentioned in the Bible; in Psalm 103:5 the poet exhorts his soul to bless God, through whose mercies "thy youth is renewed like the eagle's."

The rejuvenation of the serpent forms the basis for one of the

---

[1] See: E. Küster, *Die Schlange in der griechischen Kunst und Religion* (1913), pp. 52 f., 127 ff.; A. de Gubernatis, *Die Tiere in indogermanischer Mythologie* (1874), p. 480; J. G. Hahn, *Griechische und albanesische Märchen* (1864), vol. ii, p. 57. Pliny (x, 17) says that the enmity is due to the fact that the serpent keeps stealing the eagle's eggs.

most intriguing incidents in the Babylonian Story of Gilgamesh. While the hero was bathing, we are told, a serpent emerged from the deep and swallowed the plant of eternal youth, which Gilgamesh had left unattended in his boat. The Phoenician writer Sanchuniathon says likewise of the serpent that "it is very long-lived, and possesses the quality of sloughing its skin and assuming a second youth"; and Plutarch tells us that the same notion was current in Egypt. In Latin and Greek the same word is used for "the slough of a serpent" as for "old age"; while even today the Italians speak of "being older than a serpent" (*aver più anni d'un serpente*).

Nor is it only among ancient peoples that this belief is attested. The Wafipas of East Africa relate that God came down one day to earth and asked his creatures which of them desired to live forever. But only the serpent was awake at the time and answered; that is why it has received the privilege of sloughing its skin each year and of dying only if killed. A similar tale is told also by the Dusuns of British North Borneo: God, they say, offered immortality to any creature that could cast its skin, but only the serpent was able to do so (A 1335.5 ad.).

It is not impossible that in the original version of our tale the motive of the eagle's attack upon the hole of the serpent was, more specifically, to steal the magic plant which was in the latter's possession. This, in fact, would better explain the sequence of the story—Etana, finding that his wife is doomed to sterility on account of the curse which the gods have pronounced upon the city of Kish, appeals for some magical means of circumventing their decree and is consequently ordered to go to the eagle, who, presumably, still retains the precious plant.

Of course, by the time our present form of the story developed, this original motivation and, indeed, the real grounds for the hostility between the eagle and the serpent had long since been forgotten. The author was therefore able to build his tale around this tidbit of traditional lore without troubling himself unduly about the why and wherefore. Stories of the enmity between different animals were, in any case, familiar enough. An ancient Egyptian fable, for example, relates how the vulture and the cat plundered one another and ultimately came before the sun-god, who punished them for their breach of friendship;[2] and there are a number of Babylonian and Assyrian stories dealing with the rivalry of the wolf and the dog, and of the horse and the ox.

A curious development of our tale—or rather, of its basic theme—took place in Christian tradition, where the time-honored battle was taken to symbolize the eternal fight between good and evil, the eagle standing for the resurrected Savior, and the serpent for the wily Devil!

The second part of our story is based on the theme known to students of folklore as Borrowed Plumes (K 1041). The essence of this theme is that a presumptuous dupe lets himself be carried aloft by a bird and is eventually dropped. Variations of this story are to be found in Spain, Indonesia, Rhodesia, and among the North American Indians, while it also finds a parallel in one of the Uncle Remus stories, originally from Georgia. A variant of it is, of course, the familiar classical myth of Icarus, who fastens artificial wings upon himself, only to have them melt when he flies near the sun.

The story is full of little tidbits of popular lore which need to be explained if it is to be rendered fully intelligible.

Thus, when the shrewd eaglet warns its father that the god of justice "has a big net which covers the world, and in it he catches everyone who disobeys his laws," he is alluding to a belief which is widely attested not only among the Babylonians, but also in ancient India and even in the Bible. In the Atharvaveda, for example, it is stated that the god Varuna possesses such a mesh in

---

[2] W. Spiegelberg, *Der Aegyptische Mythus vom Sonnenauge* (1917); G. Franzow, in *Zeitschrift für Aegyptische Sprache,* vol. lxvi (1930), pp. 1 ff.

which he traps malefactors, while the anguished Job cries out to his companions (19:6), "Know now that God hath subverted my cause, and *hath compassed me with his net*." [3]

Again, when we read that seven mighty demons encircled the city of Kish and kept the gates bolted and barred, this is a reference to the ancient Mesopotamian belief in seven winds or spirits which brought disease and pestilence. They are frequently mentioned in Babylonian magical incantations, where they are said to come from the depths of the ocean or from the barren tracts of the wilderness. In the Biblical Book of Deuteronomy (28:22) the Israelite is warned that if he disobeys the commandments of Jehovah seven forms of disease "shall pursue thee until thou perish"; while a somewhat similar idea occurs in an ancient Finnish song which relates that an old woman gave birth to nine sons who were, respectively: a werewolf, a snake, a *risi*, a lizard, the nightmare, joint-ache, gout, spleen, and gripes. Her other sons were baleful monsters. [4]

A further item of popular lore may be recognized in the fact that Etana, the person chosen to be the king and savior of the doomed city, is actually a shepherd; for this plays upon the fact that among the Babylonians a regular title for the king was "shepherd of the people." The idea recurs in the Bible in the story of David who was called "from behind the sheep," just as Moses and Aaron are said to have led God's people "like a flock" (Psalm 77:21), and Cyrus is designated as the shepherd who will perform all His pleasure (Isaiah 44:28). Readers of Homer will recall that the Achaean monarchs Agamemnon and Menelaus are regularly styled "shepherds of the peoples."

Again, it is worth noting that the emblems of earthly royalty are said to be stored up in heaven. The Babylonians believed

[3] I. Scheftelowitz, *Das Schlingen- und Netzmotiv im Glauben der Völker* (1912).

[4] Jakob Grimm, *Teutonic Mythology,* translated by F. Stallybrass (1880), p. 1161.

that these were in the keeping of the supreme god Anu, who handed them to each approved sovereign in turn. It was customary to engrave upon boundary stones the symbols of the principal gods, and that of Anu is, significantly, a royal throne surmounted by the cap of sovereignty.[5] The idea is echoed in the Bible—in Psalm 110:2 the new monarch is assured that "Jehovah sends the scepter of thy prowess out of Zion, [saying], Rule thou in the midst of thine enemies!"

Lastly, a word should be said about the magic plant. The belief that conception can be induced miraculously by eating a plant or fruit—(e.g., mandrake, apple, or almond)—is well nigh universal (T 511) and appears, for instance, in the classical myth of the birth of Attis. The point of Etana's quest for such a magical plant is to circumvent the human impotence and sterility which was part of the gods' curse upon the city of Kish.

[5] Illustrations will be found in K. Frank, *Bilder und Symbole babylonisch-assyrischer Götter* (1906).

4

THE LOST CHANCE

Once upon a time Ea, the lord of wisdom and knowledge, decided, for a prank, to create a creature who would look like a man but be as wise as the gods. So down to earth he came and in the holy city of Eridu he fashioned a being whom he called Adapa. So wise was this being that nothing in heaven or earth was beyond his ken. When he opened his lips it was as if the gods themselves were speaking, and none could gainsay his words. There was no craft and no skill of which he was not the master; he could bake with the bakers and fish with the fishers and hunt with the huntsmen. And he was as good as he was wise. Pure and clean and upright, he observed all the laws of the gods; and every night, before he himself lay down to sleep, he would take care to walk around the city and see that the gates were firmly locked, so that everyone else might rest secure.

One day Adapa went out to catch fish for the repast of his master, Ea. But no sooner had he pulled away from the shore than, lo, the sky grew black, and there above his head was the great spirit of the stormwind, in the shape of a monstrous bird, sweeping the waters with its giant wings and stirring them into wild unrest. Up and down bobbed the little craft, buffeted hither and thither, until at last a mighty gust blew upon it and overturned it, and Adapa found himself struggling amid a shoal of fish.

Angrily he shook his fist in the face of the bird. Then he pronounced a solemn curse. "Stormbird," he cried, "for this I will cause your wing to be broken!" And so powerful was the curse that, scarce had it escaped his lips when the wing of the stormbird was broken.

For seven days no wind blew upon earth, and the sea was lulled into a breathless calm.

When God saw that the wind had ceased to blow, he summoned his messenger Ilabrat, the winged envoy of heaven.

"Wherefore," he asked, "has the wind ceased to blow?"

"My lord," replied the messenger, "that creature whom Ea created has broken its wing."

At these words God was very angry, and, rising from his throne, he ordered the miscreant to be brought before him.

But Ea, the wise and merciful, who knows all the secrets of heaven and from whom nothing can be hidden, came at once to the aid of his servant.

"Adapa," said he, "unbind your locks, heap ashes upon your head, and dress yourself in rags. When you reach the gate of heaven you will find two sentinels posted before it. These are the gods Tammuz and Gishzida, those two great lords of increase who vanish from the earth during the dry summer. As soon as they see you they will ask you why you are so wan and unkempt, and what brings you in such guise to the gate of heaven.

" 'Two gods have vanished from the earth,' you must answer, 'and I am come to mourn for them and to entreat the mercy of God.'

"By these words you will win their hearts, and they will spring to your aid and plead your cause before the heavenly judge. Then God's anger will be cooled, and he will order food and drink to be set before you. But the food you must not eat, for it is food of death; and the water you must not drink, for it is water of death. Only when they offer you clean raiment and oil may you safely accept. Heed my words and forget them not!"

Thereupon Adapa did as Ea had told him. He unbound his locks and heaped ashes upon his head and dressed himself in rags.

Presently the messenger of God arrived. "Adapa," he cried, "is charged with breaking the wing of the stormbird. Let him be brought forth to judgment!"

So Adapa was delivered into the hands of the messenger, to be brought before the heavenly court.

When he reached the gate of heaven there were two sentinels posted before it, even as Ea had said.

"Halt!" they cried, barring his path. "What brings you to the court of heaven in such guise as this?"

But Adapa was ready with his answer. "Two great gods," said he, "have vanished from the earth. I am come to mourn them and to entreat the mercy of God."

"And who might they be?" asked the sentries.

"Tammuz and Gishzida," replied Adapa.

At these words the hearts of the sentries melted, and they spoke gently to Adapa and ushered him into the presence of God.

Then God rose from his throne and called in a loud and terrible voice, "Adapa, stand forth and answer! Why did you break the stormbird's wing?"

But Adapa was undismayed. "Sire," he replied calmly, "it happened in this wise. Ea, the lord of wisdom, had made me wise beyond all men and bared to me the secrets of heaven and earth. So I resolved to render him thanks by providing him daily with food. One day I went down upon the ocean to catch fish for his dinner. When I launched my boat the sea was like a mirror, and no ripple stirred upon it. But, all of a sudden the stormbird came swooping down and whipped the waters into wild unrest, and presently my craft overturned, and my master was left to go hungry. At this I was so incensed that I pronounced a curse upon it and caused its wing to be broken."

While he spoke God peered at him intently, his chin cupped in his hand, unable to make up his mind whether or not to believe him. But no sooner had Adapa finished than at once Tammuz and Gishzida sprang forward and bowed themselves low before the heavenly throne.

"Lord God," they cried, "Adapa speaks the truth. No impious varlet is he, but one who is mindful of the gods and loves them. For behold, even now, when his own life hangs in the balance, he is come before thee with locks unbound and in the garb of a mourner to grieve over us and entreat thy grace. We beseech thee, O Lord, account not his deed for unrighteousness, and condemn him not!"

At these words God's anger was calmed, and his heart was moved. "Adapa," said he, turning to the gods all about him, "is free of guilt and shall not be punished."

Then he paused for a moment and puckered his brow. "Moreover," he continued presently, "since Ea has made him the peer of the gods, mere mortal though he seems to be, let him henceforth rank as a god! Set before him food and water that he may eat and drink of our fare and so become one of ourselves!"

But when they set the food and water before him Adapa remembered the words of Ea and would neither eat nor drink.

"Ah," said God, smiling to himself, "so Adapa is a man after all—purblind, foolish, unwise! For, see, he refuses the food and drink which would make him immortal!"

Then he turned to his servants. "Take him away," he commanded, "and let him return to the earth!"

But God is kind and gracious, and he remembered the righteousness of Adapa and how Adapa had walked in piety before him.

"Adapa," he said gently, "although you must now go back to earth, yet shall you have your reward." And he showed him all the mysteries of heaven and all its glory and wonder.

Then he rose up on his throne and pronounced a decree. "Although," said he, "Adapa must now return to earth, he shall not be heir to mortal ills. The mighty Ninkarrak, the Lady of Healing, shall be ever at his side. If sickness comes nigh him, she shall cause it to depart. If pestilence approaches him, she shall turn it aside. If disaster heads toward him, she shall stand in its path. If ever he lies down troubled and sleepless, she shall soothe him and bring him ease. Moreover, he shall be a lord of men, and his heirs shall be kings forever, and the city of Eridu, where he lives, shall be the fief of no man!"

And so it was, and so it is. For the children of Adapa sit upon the throne even unto this day, and the city of Eridu pays fief to none.

Comment

"The Lost Chance" or "The Story of Adapa," has been known for over fifty years, but although it has been translated and discussed many times, it is doubtful whether its real point has been properly grasped. That point is that *Adapa is not a human being,* so that the theme of the story is not—as has been generally thought—man's loss of immortality. On the contrary, he is a special kind of creature, fashioned as a prank by the god Ea—neither man nor god, but something betwixt and between, possessing the form of the one and the intelligence of the other.

Only on this basis—and it is clearly stated in the original text—does the story become intelligible. Now we understand, for one thing, how Adapa can be in possession of a magic spell powerful enough to break the wings of the wind. And now we understand also the real purport of the supreme god's decision when Adapa is brought to trial before him. When that god becomes convinced that Adapa really acted out of piety he is prepared to admit him to the full status of godhead and therefore offers him the food and drink of heaven, consumption of which would automatically confer godhead upon him. But it is just this eventuality that Ea has cunningly foreseen. He does not want his special creature to be translated to the gods, for then his services would be lost, and the prank would prove a boomerang. He has therefore persuaded Adapa that such fare would really be the food of death. When God sees that the creature swallows this nonsense instead of the viands, it becomes clear to him that Adapa is indeed more mortal than divine. "So Adapa is man after all," he exclaims, "purblind, foolish, unwise!" And therewith he orders him to be returned to the earth.

But Adapa is not entirely a man, and it is in recognition of this that God supplements his judgment with a further decree: though the creature is to dwell in the world of men, he is to be immune from all the ills to which mortal flesh is heir. Excluded from the company of heaven, he is nonetheless to be something more than human.

All of this is not to imply, of course, that the author may not have drawn for his purpose upon the well-known motif of the Perverted Message (A 1335.1) the theme of which is that man forfeits immortality because a divine message telling him how to obtain it is malevolently perverted by the messenger. This motif is common through the world, the messenger being often represented as an animal, especially a serpent. Sir James Frazer has even suggested that it may underlie the story of the Temptation and Fall in the Book of Genesis.[1] The point is, however, that even if our author did have such traditional lore in mind, it was only by way of vague reminiscence. At best, all he used were the bare contours of the story, for the theme and direction of his narrative are entirely different.

The scholarly priests of Eridu, who preserved the tale, had, of course, to tint it with their own colors. The learned, wise, and pious Adapa had perforce to be represented as the prime ancestor of the royal household, while the traditional status of the shrine as a "free city," exempt from feudal taxation, had likewise to be made part and parcel of the reward bestowed on him by God. Such churchly and scholastic embellishments of a popular tale are, of course, by no means uncommon, and are readily recognized for what they are. By a similar absurd elaboration, a late Assyrian text ascribes a medical prescription to Adapa, evidently on the grounds that the man who was himself immune from

---

[1] Sir James G. Frazer, *Folklore in the Old Testament* (London: Macmillan & Co., Ltd., 1919), vol. i, pp. 52 ff.; O. Dänhardt, *Natursagen* (1907–12), vol. iii, p. 22.

sickness might be admirably qualified to act as physician to his fellows!

It remains only to add a few words about the concept of the stormbird. In several mythologies winds and thunder are thought to be caused by the flapping of the wings of a giant eagle or similar bird of prey (A 284.2). The Sumerians had such a figure in the monster Im-Dugud, while in India it was the eagle Garuda and in the Eddas the monstrous Hraesvelgr. The belief is attested also among the Chinese, the Burmese, the Finns and Shetland Islanders, the Tlingits, the Aztecs, and the inhabitants of Vancouver Island. The "wings of the wind" are likewise mentioned in the Bible, namely, in Psalms 18:11 and 104:3.

5

HOW TOOTHACHE
CAME INTO THE WORLD

After God had created heaven,
heaven created earth;
earth created rivers;
rivers created ditches;
ditches created mud;
mud created the worm.

But the worm had nothing to eat.
So he went to the god of justice
and wept and wept;
and before Ea, the god of wisdom,
he poured forth his tears.

"What will you give me to eat?" he cried,
"and what will you give me to drink?"

"I will give you ripe figs," said the god of justice,
"and I will give you apricots."

"What good are ripe figs?" cried the worm.
"And what use are apricots?

Lift me up from the mud
and place me among men's teeth,
and set me down in their jaws,
that I may drink the blood of their teeth
and feed on the roots of their jaws!"

"Very well," said the god of justice.
"You have made your choice.
You may lie among men's teeth;
you may lie among their jaws.
But henceforth and for evermore
the mighty hand of Ea shall be against you to crush you!"

> *And so it has remained. The worm preys upon the teeth and gnaws at the gums of men; but the dentist, the servant of Ea, attacks him and kills him.*
>
> *And that is not all. Whenever you have a toothache and you brew a drug to ease it, recite this story thrice, and you will surely be cured.*

Comment

The idea that toothache is caused by a worm is well nigh universal. It is found already in the Homeric "Hymn to Demeter," which dates approximately from the fifth century B.C.,[1] and it is current also in the popular lore of China, India, Finland, and Scotland—to mention only a few instances.[2] Shakespeare alludes

---

[1] Lines 228–29.
[2] See: William Crooke, *Popular Religion and Folklore of North India* (Westminster, England: A. Constable & Co., 1896), vol. i, p. 151; John Abercromby,

to it in *Much Ado about Nothing* (Act III, Scene ii, 21 ff.), where Benedick complains, "I have a toothache," only to be rebuked by his friends with the words, "What! sigh for a toothache, where is but a humour or a worm?" [3] R. Campbell Thompson, the scholar who first published our Assyrian tale, informs us that the belief has always obtained in Mesopotamia; [4] and it survives, indeed, in our own day, when we speak of a toothache as "a *gnawing* pain" or when the German says, *"Es wurmt mich"* (The worm has got me).

So common, indeed, was this notion that sometimes the application of a worm was actually recommended as a means of removing decayed teeth without the pain of surgery. Thus Pliny the Elder (23–79 A.D.) assures us in his *Natural History* that "in the plant called spelt there is a worm similar to the wood-fretter. If this be put with wax into the hollow of a decayed tooth, that tooth will come out"; [5] while elsewhere in the same work he observes that "ashes of burnt earthworms, or a live cabbage caterpillar, introduced into carious teeth make them come out easily." [6] The same remedy is prescribed again, some five hundred years later, by the physician Aetius of Amida; while even in the seventeenth century the *Fairfax Household Recipe Book* recommends the following method of treatment: "Take worms when they be a-gendering together. Dry them upon a hot tile-stone; then make powder of them, and what tooth ye touch with it will fall out." [7]

Pre- and Protohistoric Finns (London: D. Nutt, 1898), vol. i, p. 328; *Scottish County Folklore*, vol. iii (Orkneys), p. 140; *Notes and Queries*, vol. xxiv (1876), pp. 155, 476; vol. xxvi (1877), p. 97; George Lyman Kittredge, *Witchcraft in Old and New England* (Cambridge, Mass.: Harvard University Press, 1929), p. 36; T. W. Allen, W. R. Halliday, and E. E. Sikes, *The Homeric Hymns* (Oxford: Clarendon Press, 1936), p. 156.

[3] See T. F. Thistleton-Dyer, *Folk Lore of Shakespeare* (New York: E. P. Dutton & Co., 1883), pp. 273 f.

[4] *Proceedings of the Society of Biblical Archaeology,* vol. xxviii (1906), p. 78.

[5] XXII, 51.

[6] XXX, 8.

[7] See B. R. Townend, "Non-Surgical Removal of Teeth—A Historical Survey," in *The British Dental Journal,* November 19, 1938.

It needs only to be added, for the clarification of the story, that the reason why Ea, the god of wisdom, is introduced is that he was regarded also as the master of all sciences, including medicine. Ea was thought to live in the deep, because water was deemed essential for magical and medicinal practices. (Indeed, the word for "physician" in most of the Semitic languages comes from an ancient Sumerian term which really means "conversant with water.") The chief seat of his worship was Eridu (modern Abu Shahrein), reputedly the oldest city of Babylonia, which lay on the bank of the Euphrates (west of its present course), near the Persian Gulf. This was a prominent center of magic and sorcery.

HITTITE STORIES

6

THE GOD
WHO DISAPPEARED

Once upon a time the great god Telipinu, who brings fertility
to the earth, fell into a temper because of the wicked ways
of men and decided to go into hiding. So angry was he that
he could not even stop to put on his boots aright, but, clamp-
ing his right boot on to his left foot and his left boot on to his
right foot, he stalked off in high dudgeon.

Immediately everything on earth went out of balance. It
seemed as though springtime and summer would never
come. Out of doors the rivers and lakes remained frozen, and
the snow refused to thaw. All the trees were bare, and in the
fields not a single blade of grass appeared. In the stalls and
barns the sheep and oxen huddled together, and in the houses
men crowded around the hearth until the ashes were
mountain-high, and it was impossible to look out of the
windows because they were covered with soot and smoke. So
cold was it, to boot, that no one could leave the house to
empty the refuse or to get food, and all the world was threatened with grievous famine.

All life seemed, indeed, to have come to a standstill. The
sheep rejected the ram, and the cow the bull; and even those

beasts which were already heavy with young refused to give birth.

When the sun-god, who surveys all things and whose eye is upon all, saw what was happening, he summoned all the rest of the gods and goddesses to a banquet. After they had regaled themselves on the lavish fare which he provided, and had drunk down copious draughts of wine and strong drink, he laid the trouble squarely before them.

"My son Telipinu," said he, "has disappeared from the earth. He has flown into a temper and taken himself off, but along with himself he has taken away all goodness and increase!"

When they heard these words the gods great and small at once began to search for their brother. Up hill and down dale they searched, over the mountains and along the rivers, but though they sought him high and low, they could not find him.

Back they came to the sun-god and told him of their failure.

Then the sun-god sent out a swift and sharp-eyed eagle. "Search the high mountains," he commanded, "and search the deep valleys, and whenever you espy swirling waters, gaze intently into them, for maybe Telipinu has been trapped by them."

So the eagle went and flew over the high mountains and swooped down upon the deep valleys, and whenever it espied swirling waters it gazed intently into them; but however far it flew and however intently it gazed, Telipinu was nowhere to be found.

So back the eagle came to the sun-god and told him of its failure.

Meanwhile the earth was continuing to languish, and now it seemed that not only men but the gods also were in dire plight; for if the beasts should die and there be no crops, they too would be deprived of the offerings upon which they lived.

At this thought, they were sore dismayed and began to wring their hands and to pace up and down in anguish.

Now there was one god who was especially wild and impetuous. This was the god of the winds—a god who could never keep still but was usually to be found rushing hither and yon, roaring and bellowing, huffing and puffing.

"Why," cried he, "we shall all of us die of hunger. Something must be done!"

"Indeed," replied his mother, the beneficent queen of the gods, "something must surely be done. But go and do it yourself! You are a mighty and powerful god, and you drive all things before you. You can reach into the darkest cavern, and you whistle down every nook and cranny. You rustle the leaves and stir the streams and shake men's houses, and when you blow upon the fields all the cornstalks bow before you. Go yourself and seek Telipinu!"

So the god of the winds went forth over all the earth, until at last he came to a city where Telipinu was wont to lodge. "Maybe," thought he to himself, "he is still here after all." So he knocked on the gate, but there was no response. Then, with his full force, he rushed against it until it fell from its hinges. But Telipinu was nowhere to be found.

Thereupon the god of the winds returned to heaven, full of chagrin and dismay, and sat down in silence. And no breeze rustled and no zephyr stirred, and everywhere there was a breathless hush.

But woman's wit is sharper than the wind, and keener, and when the queen of heaven saw that none of the mighty gods—even the wind himself—had been able to find Telipinu, she resolved to take matters into her own hands. So she summoned to herself a tiny bee.

"Little bee," said she, "go and seek Telipinu! When you find him, put your sting into his hands and feet. Then he will surely bestir himself; and when he has bestirred himself, smear him with your wax and bring him to me!"

When he heard the goddess thus addressing the bee, the wind felt sore at heart and affronted. "Why," cried he, with mocking laughter, "the gods great and small have searched for Telipinu and found him not. Think you that this tiny bee, with its weak little wings, will be able to succeed where they have failed?"

"Have done!" replied the goddess brusquely. "It will surely go and find him!"

So away sped the bee, buzzing over the high mountains, humming over the deep valleys, droning over the paths of the rivers. At last, when all its honey was well nigh drained from weakness, and all its strength beginning to fail, it came to a clearing in a forest beside the city of Lihzina and, lo and behold, there, fast asleep upon his back, lay none other than Telipinu himself!

In less time than it takes to tell, the little bee had placed its sting in Telipinu's hands and feet, and presently the god stirred and awoke. But gods are like men when they are rudely roused from their slumbers, and Telipinu was in a towering rage.

"Why," he stormed, "do you have to come disturbing me? Can't you see that I am trying to sleep? And don't you know that when anyone has the sulks as I have he is better left alone? Do you think I am in the mood for a chat?"

Indeed, Telipinu was even more angry than he had been before, and no sooner had he got to his feet and started striding down the path than he proceeded to destroy everything he met. The rivers, which before had been but frozen over, now dried out completely, and springs, where they had at least been a trickle, failed altogether.

But the bee, though among the smallest of creatures, is yet among the wisest, and knew what to do. With all that remained of its strength it returned straightway to the goddess.

"I have found Telipinu," it reported, "but I alone cannot bring him back, for he will have to be carried over the lofty peaks of Amanus and over the steep falls, and that is beyond my strength. Let an eagle accompany me. I will show it where the god lies, and it can bear him aloft on its wing!"

Thereupon the goddess summoned an eagle and told it to go forth along with the bee and bring Telipinu back.

"But that," she added, "is only the first step. He is still furious and in a temper, and it will need high magic both in heaven and on earth to drive out his wrath!"

Across the hills and over the dales flew the eagle and the bee, while the gods clustered about the ramparts of heaven, waiting with bated breath for the moment of their return.

It was a long and anxious wait, but at last what seemed like a small black cloud rolled up on the horizon; and even as it appeared there was a rumble of thunder and a flash of lightning, and the air was rent with loud and angry cries.

The gods huddled together.

Louder and louder grew the thunder, more strident the cries, more dazzling and more frequent the lightning, until it seemed as though heaven and earth were locked in combat.

Suddenly, above the din and clamor, came the steady drone of a bee in flight, and the black cloud began to take on a familiar shape. When the gods looked closer, there, winging toward them, was the eagle, with Telipinu poised upon its pinion, and the little bee buzzing and humming around it, partly in triumph, partly in fear.

In a few moments the bird had alighted, and immediately a train of servants moved forward, bearing in their hands goblets of nectar, jars of cream and honey, and baskets of fruit; and as they set them before Telipinu the great goddess Kamrusepa stood beside them and made sweet music, crooning over each a little snatch of song.

Over the figs she sang:

> "Bitter figs turn sweet with age.
> Be turn'd to sweet thy bitter rage!"

And over the grapes and olives:

> "As the olive's with oil, the grape's with wine,
> With grace be fill'd that heart of thine!"

And over the cream and honey:

> "Be smooth as cream, as honey sweet.
> Now from thine angry mood retreat!"

Although they sounded to Telipinu like prayers and petitions, these words were really magic spells—for Kamrusepa was the mistress of the black art—and so no sooner had the angry god tasted a few bites of the food and quaffed a few sips of the drink than he was instantly bewitched. All the rage and fury which had been seething within him seemed of a sudden to vanish, and in its place there stole over him a warm and gentle glow of benevolence. The more he ate and the more he drank, the more kindly he became, for every time the enchanted fare touched his lips grace abounding entered his soul.

At length, when the gods saw that his anger had altogether departed and that he was filled with love and tenderness toward them, they redecked the tables and replaced the benches and resumed the banquet which had been so rudely interrupted. There they sat as before, feasting and carousing —the gods of field, crop, and grain, and the goddesses of birth and of fate—but now, in the center, sat Telipinu himself, gaily receiving and returning their toasts.

Meanwhile, down on earth, mortals too were bestirring themselves to remove the god's displeasure, but because of the blight and the famine they could not offer him food and drink, as did his brothers and sisters in heaven. So in every house they flung open the doors and windows and chanted in chorus:

> "Out of the house and thro' the window,
>   Out of the window and thro' the yard,
>   Out of the yard and thro' the gate,
>   Out of the gate and down the path
>   Go the fury, the rage, the wrath!
>
> Down the path and straight ahead,
>   Nor turn aside to garden-bed
>   Or field or orchard-close, but hie
>   To where the earth doth meet the sky,
>   And, like the setting sun at night,
>   Sink and disappear from sight!"

Then someone brought a large bowl of gruel and stirred it vigorously with a wooden spoon, while all the others shouted in chorus:

> "Stir around, and stir around,
>   Till no lumps herein be found.
>   Stir thy spirit, stir thy heart,
>   Till their roughnesses depart!"

Finally they washed and scoured the insides of their houses and then tossed the pails of sullied water upon the stones, while they sang:

> "Water pour'd upon the floor
>   To the pail returns no more.
>   Pour the temper from thy heart,
>   Likewise let it now depart!"

Now although they sounded to Telipinu like prayers and petitions, the words they chanted were also really magic spells, and suddenly the cold winter winds seemed to abate, and through the open doors and windows stole the first breezes of spring. On the branches of the trees and in the hedgerows a promise of green began to appear and, as if in a moment, field and woodland were alive with a thousand sounds—the purling of brooks, the scampering of tiny feet, the first hesitant notes of fledgling birds.

A few days later a tall pole was set up in the courtyard of the temple, and from it was hung, in honor of Telipinu, the snow-white fleece of a newborn lamb.

Comment

Ancient peoples accounted for the barren season of the year by supposing that the god or goddess of fertility then descended into the nether regions or otherwise withdrew from the earth. The Babylonians, for example, told this story of their god Tammuz, whom they lamented annually in midsummer, while the Syrians related it of the analogous figure of Adonis,

> Whose annual wound in Lebanon allur'd
> The Syrian damsels to lament his fate
> In amorous ditties all a summer's day,
> While smooth Adonis from his native rock
> Ran purple to the sea, suppos'd with blood
> Of Tammuz yearly wounded.[1]

Similarly the Greeks told it of Persephone, who spent six months of each year in the netherworld:

> She waits for each and other,
> She waits for all men born;
> Forgets the earth her mother,
> The life of fruits and corn;
> And spring and seed and swallow
> Take wing for her and follow
> Where summer song rings hollow,
> And flowers are put to scorn.[2]

The story of Telipinu, the god who disappeared, is simply a variation on the same theme.

Since we know from other sources that Telipinu was the

---

[1] John Milton, *Paradise Lost,* Book I, 447–52.
[2] Algernon Charles Swinburne, "The Garden of Proserpine."

subject of periodic "wailings," it is not improbable that our story was originally designed for the festival at which those wailings took place, and that it was recited as an accompaniment to the ceremonies of that occasion. In that case, the elaborate rites of exorcism which are so prominent a feature of it may well reflect and project the widespread custom of banishing evil and expelling demons at the moment (e.g., New Year's Day) when the new lease of life is thought to be beginning.[3] The Hebrews, for instance, prefaced the opening of the agricultural year with the solemn rite of expelling a scapegoat and purifying both the people and the sacred vessels.[4] The Romans scoured the temples for a full month before the beginning of the year in March— wherefore, indeed, that month was called February, or "Scouring." [5] Similarly, in Siam, the forces of evil and the powers of darkness are expelled on the last day of the year; [6] and among the tribes of Hindu Kush they are driven out immediately after the harvest has been reaped.[7] At Cape Coast Castle a demon named Abonsam is expelled annually after a four-week period of mortification; [8] and among the Ashanti the entire nation is purified and the king reconsecrated at the feast of Odwira, or Purgation, in September, when the shrines also are cleansed.[9] A survival of such rites may be seen, in fact, in our own custom of "spring cleaning," and in the ringing of bells and clanging of gongs on New Year's Eve.

Although our present version of the tale was evidently designed for recitation or performance at a public seasonal festival, fragments of other versions have also come down to us, in which

[3] Cf. T. H. Gaster, *Thespis* (New York: 1950), pp. 17–20.
[4] Leviticus 16.
[5] Joh. Lydus, *De mensibus*, iv, 25.
[6] J. G. Frazer, *The Golden Bough* (New York: The Macmillan Company, 1951), p. 559.
[7] Ibid., p. 557.
[8] Ibid., p. 555.
[9] C. G. Seligman, *Races of Africa* (1930), pp. 71–72.

the narrative is adapted for use in more private and domestic rituals. In these the angry god is not Telipinu but the patron deity of a particular household; the cause of his anger is not the general wickedness of mankind but the special guilt of a single person; and the effect of his withdrawal is not a blight upon the earth but, more exclusively, upon the guilty person's produce or household.[10] In one case, for example, the culprit seems to have been an early Hittite queen named Asmunikkal.[11] The recitation of the tale evidently formed part of the ceremonies designed to remove the disaster and win back the favor of the outraged god.

Of especial interest is the role assigned in our story to the bee. When all the gods fail to rouse the dormant Telipinu, the bee is sent out, brings him to his feet by stinging him, and then cleanses him with its wax. It may be suggested that the basis of this incident lies not only in its dramatic quality but also in the common belief that the sting of a bee can cure paralysis of the limbs, or "stitch," [12] and that its wax or honey is a powerful agent capable of expelling evil spirits from the body and of accomplishing rejuvenation.[13] In the Finnish Kalevala the hero Lemminkäinen, after he has been bitten by a serpent and cut in pieces by his enemies, is reanimated only when a bee, sent out by his mother, fetches special honey from the ninth heaven. Similarly, in the ancient pseudepigraphical work entitled *The Life and Confession of Asenath, the Wife of Joseph,* the archangel Michael miraculously provides that Egyptian princess with a honeycomb by the use of which she achieves not only purification but also immortality.

[10] Cf. H. Otten, *Die Uberlieferungen des Telipinu-Mythus* (1942), pp. 49 ff.
[11] Ibid., p. 60.
[12] B. F. Beck, *Honey and Health* (1938), pp. 96, 101; J. Jühling, *Die Tiere in der deutschen Volksmedizin* (1900), pp. 88 f.
[13] Beck, op. cit., pp. 209 ff.; W. M. Roscher, *Nektar und Ambrosia* (1883), pp. 46 ff.; *Encyclopaedia of Religion and Ethics,* vi, p. 770; H. M. Ransome, *The Sacred Bee* (1937).

7

THE MONSTER
MADE OF STONE

Long, long ago, at the very beginning of the world, there reigned in heaven a mighty god named Alalu. For nine whole years he sat upon his throne in peace, while his vizier Anu stood before him, ready to perform his least behest. But in the tenth year Anu rebelled and, driving his master from the throne, seized it for himself.

For nine whole years Anu sat upon his throne in peace, while his vizier Kumarbi stood before him, ready to perform his least behest. But in the tenth year Kumarbi rebelled and challenged his master to battle.

Fast and furious raged the fight, until at last, as Anu was turning to flee from his grasp, Kumarbi bit him savagely in the loins and swallowed some of his seed.

"Aha," he said, chuckling, "now you are in my power! For see, I have unmanned you, and now you will have no sons to succeed you!"

"Laugh not too soon," replied his rival. "For what you have swallowed will grow within you into three great and terrible beings, furious as the Tigris in full flood, wild as the raging wind, relentless as the god of battle! Like the swirling streams and the angry blasts, they will dash you in the end against the rocks!"

At these words Kumarbi was filled with terror and tried at once to spit out that which he had swallowed. But only a small portion of it came forth from his mouth and, behold, it alighted at Mount Kanzura, the dwelling of the gods. And when the gods saw what had happened they were seized with alarm.

Kumarbi was now thoroughly dismayed, for he was ashamed to show himself before his brethren in this strange and sorry condition. So away he hied, down from the courts of heaven to the earthly city of Nippur, and there he established his dwelling. Then he began to count the months until the monstrous offspring should come to birth.

In the seventh month Anu, who was hiding in heaven, called suddenly to the monsters and bade them come forth from the body of Kumarbi.

"Come forth through his mouth," he cried.

"Nay," replied the monsters, "that can we not do. For we are not mere lifeless lumps. The gods have now given us strength and vigor and mind and heart; were we to come forth in such fashion, well might we be maimed and damaged!"

"Then come forth through his ears," cried Anu.

"That too would not be safe," rejoined the monsters. "That too might well impair us!"

"Then find some suitable place from which you may indeed come forth," screamed the god in desperation.

But there was no such place in the whole of Kumarbi's body.

Anu was now greatly dismayed, for it seemed that the

monsters would never come forth and that he would never be avenged and win back the throne.

"There is only one thing to do," thought he. "I must go to Ea, the lord of wisdom, and seek his counsel and aid."

So away he went to Ea and laid the matter before him. "Master of all knowledge," said he, "in the body of Kumarbi lie two mighty monsters, fruit of my seed, upon whom I am relying to avenge me and win back for me my throne. But lo, these monsters are imprisoned and cannot come forth!"

"Never fear," replied Ea benignly, "for naught is beyond my skill, and I shall surely bring them to birth."

Thereupon he spake softly to the monsters and bade them once more to come forth through the mouth or ears of Kumarbi. But the monsters merely repeated what they had said to Anu.

"Then find some suitable place," cried the god, "from which you may indeed come forth!"

But again the monsters refused.

When Ea saw that he could not persuade them and that the cause of Anu appeared to be doomed, he took a great knife and, while Kumarbi lay fast asleep, he cut a hole in the giant frame, even as a man might split a stone.

Out of the body of Kumarbi sprang the mighty god Desire. But the other of the two monsters remained imprisoned within it.

One day Kumarbi was out for a walk when whom should he meet coming toward him but Ea himself? At the sight of the god Kumarbi bowed low to the ground. Then he began to entreat him.

"Lord Ea," he cried, "with thee is all wisdom and knowledge. Come to my aid, for, behold, I carry within me a burden which I cannot support."

But Ea paid no heed to his words and, smiling wryly, passed upon his way.

Heavier and heavier grew the weight of the monster within the body of Kumarbi, and greater and greater grew his torment and despair. At last, when he could endure it no longer, he betook himself to that mighty goddess, the Lady of Green Things, in whose hands are all cures and simples and every plant of healing.

"Sweet goddess," he cried, falling at her feet and clutching the hem of her robe, "I beseech thee, grant me a boon. Give me a herb to ease my distress and to relieve me of this burden, that I may confound him who has sought to confound me, who has brought me to labor like a woman and filled my belly with the east wind!"

Then the goddess fetched a herb from her garden and gave it to Kumarbi. "Eat this," she said, "and all will be well."

But there was a quizzical smile on her lips, and no sooner had Kumarbi tasted the herb than all of a sudden his mouth began to twitch and his teeth to ache. Then he knew that the goddess had deceived him and made sport of him and, wincing and shrieking with pain, he fled to Ea and again besought his aid.

But Ea merely smiled. "You can see for yourself," said he, "that there is now no other way. You must be delivered like a woman. Summon a skillful midwife, and bid all the lords and nobles and all the magicians and sorcerers come to your mansion and attend the birth!"

So a skillful midwife was summoned, and all the lords and nobles and all the magicians and sorcerers gathered at

Kumarbi's mansion to attend the birth of the monstrous child. Music was played, spells were chanted, and magic rites were performed; and at length from the loins of that great god sprang the infant spirit of the wind. . . .

Meanwhile Anu was waiting impatiently in heaven. As soon as he heard the child had been born he resolved to win it over to his cause.

One day, when the child was fully grown, he was out walking in the cool of the evening when suddenly he came upon an old man sitting by the roadside, muttering and mumbling to himself, and every now and again he seemed to let fall a name which sounded like Kumarbi.

For several moments the lad stood staring at the curious sight. Then he approached softly and tapped the stranger on the arm. "Grandfather," he said, "what is amiss? What is your name, and who is distressing you?"

The old man lifted his head and gazed steadily into the face of the lad. "My son," he said slowly, "I am the god Anu. For nine long years I sat in peace upon the throne of heaven; and Kumarbi, my vizier, stood before me, ready to perform my least behest. But in the tenth year he rebelled and drove me from my dominion and unmanned me. Now I have no son to succeed me, and a stranger will sit in my place. I beseech you, do battle against this tyrant and avenge me!"

When he heard these words the lad was moved to pity and resolved at once to do battle for the hapless god. So he mounted his chariot and urged on the heavenly bull which drew it, and made ready to go forth into the fray.

But the bull would not move. "Wherefore," it cried, "would you pit your strength against the mighty gods? For behold, they are mustered to do battle for Kumarbi. There is the sun-god and the god of war, and there too are all the great lords of heaven. How can you hope to subdue them?"

"A fig for them all!" retorted the youth. "A fig for the lord of wisdom and the sun-god and the god of war! Cursed be all who would curse me!"

And therewith he took hold on the reins and lashed the bull and set out to do battle.

Fierce and furious was the fight as the storm-god unleashed his blasts against the hosts of heaven, but at length Kumarbi was worsted and driven forth; and once again the mighty Anu sat in peace upon his throne.

For a long while Kumarbi lay nursing his wounds and plotting revenge. At last he devised a cunning plan. So he summoned Impaluri, the trusted vizier of the lord of the sea, and sent him post-haste to his master.

"My lord," said the messenger, "come at once. Kumarbi has something to discuss with you."

At these words the lord of the sea grew very frightened. "Perhaps," thought he, "Kumarbi imagines I am on the side of his enemies, and is minded to take vengeance upon me."

"Return," he replied, "and say emphatically to Kumarbi that there is no need for him to be angry against me or my household and to strike terror and panic into us. We remain his loyal servants. We have prepared a banquet for him, and the minstrels stand ready. Let him come and join us."

So Kumarbi went to the house of the lord of the sea and partook of the banquet. Presently, when the wine was flowing freely and everyone was in a mellow mood, he felt emboldened to broach his request.

"Lord of the Sea," he said, "I am in a bitter plight and have need of your help. The spirit of the wind has driven me from the throne and put back upon it my hated rival Anu. All of the gods have rallied to his side and no longer give me obedience. Yet I can see no way to defeat him."

The lord of the sea stroked his beard and bowed his head in thought. At last he looked up, and there was a mischievous glint in his eye.

"Kumarbi," he said, "I have a plan. Go at once to the mountain. Lie down upon it and pour your seed into it. Within a few months the mountain will bring forth a child made of stone. As soon as it is born, carry it secretly to the abyss beneath the depths of the sea, and place it on the right shoulder of Upelluri, the giant who dwells therein and who supports the weight of earth and heaven. Day by day it will grow taller and taller, until at last its head will strike the floor of heaven, and all the gods will be toppled from their thrones and flee in dismay. Thus you will be able to regain your dominion."

When the lord of the sea had finished, Kumarbi at once sent for his messenger Mukishanu and told him to go down to the waters and command their obedience in carrying out the plan of their master, the lord of the sea.

The next morning, as soon as the sun was up, he journeyed to the mountain and lay down upon it and poured his seed into it.

Within a few months the mountain began to writhe and quake, and when the heavenly nurses saw what was happening, they hastened toward it to assist at the birth, and with them came also the weird sisters to pronounce the destiny of the newborn child.

Long and hard the mountain travailed, until at last there sprang from it a huge boulder shaped like a human babe. At once the goddesses sprang forward to receive it, carried it tenderly to Kumarbi, and placed it upon his knees.

Kumarbi was beside himself with joy. Taking the child in his arms, he lifted it high into the air and dandled it upon his lap, while he crooned:

> "Baby, baby, grow so high,
> Till your shoulders touch the sky.
> Rock the clouds, and down will fall
> Storm-god, storm-god's hosts, and all,
> Flitter-flutter, like a bird
> Fleeing when its nest is stirred!"

But even as he was singing the child stretched out its hand to a vase which was lying on a table nearby, and with a sudden sweep sent it crashing in splinters to the floor. Kumarbi was unperturbed. "This," thought he, "is an omen." And without a pause he continued:

> "Afterward to Kummi go;
> Smite it, raze it, lay it low.
> Crush the gods that there be found,
> Like shatter'd pots upon the ground!"

At last he stopped and set the child firmly upon his knee and gazed intently into its stony, unsmiling face. "Baby," he said, "I must give you a name. You shall be called Ullikummi. For whenever men hear that name in days to come they will bethink them of the city of Kummi, the earthly abode of the storm-god, and they will remember how you laid it low."

Then Kumarbi sent for Impaluri and bade him fetch the

faery maidens who bring newborn children into the world.

"Maidens," he said when they arrived, "take this child and carry it down to the abyss beneath the depths of the sea, and place it on the right shoulder of Upelluri. May it grow by the yard and by the furlong and by the mile and shoot up like a giant pillar until it reaches the sky!"

But when the faery maidens looked upon the child and saw that it was made of stone, they were filled with dismay and decided first to show it to Enlil, the mighty god of Nippur, and to seek his advice. As soon, however, as Enlil set eyes upon it, he shrank back in alarm.

"No ordinary child is this," he cried. "No goddess blessed its birth, and no fate sang over its cradle. This is no babe, but a monster—a monster devised by Kumarbi as a match for the spirit of the winds!"

Nevertheless, the maidens felt bound by the command of Kumarbi, and down they went to the abyss beneath the depths of the sea, and placed the creature upon the right shoulder of Upelluri, the giant who supports earth and heaven.

Well, the creature grew and grew, shooting forth like a shaft making straight for the target. In fifteen days the waters came up only to its waist, and presently only to its knees. . . .

One day, when the sun had climbed, as was his wont, to the topmost crag of Mount Hazzi,* the tallest mountain in the whole of Syria, he chanced to rest awhile and stood gazing down into the ocean below. Suddenly his eyes rested upon a wondrous sight, for there, shooting up out of the waters, was a giant pillar, growing higher by the

* This is the classical Mons Casius, modern Jebel el-Akra.

minute, until its head nigh touched the floor of heaven.

Quickening his pace, the sun-god rushed at once to the spirit of the winds to tell him what he had seen. By the time he arrived he was tired and forspent with the long journey, and the spirit of the winds ordered his minister Tasmisu to regale him with food and drink. But the sun-god was far too excited to taste them, and in broken, halting words he poured out his story of the strange apparition.

Scarcely believing his ears, the spirit of the winds at once summoned his minister to his side, and they made ready to set out whither the sun-god led. And as soon as their sister Ishtar saw what was afoot, she too came forth from her bower and joined them.

Long and weary was the road, and when at last they reached the topmost crag of the mountain and gazed down upon the ocean below, they saw, rising out of the waters, the giant pillar, growing higher by the minute, its head nearly touching the floor of heaven.

At the sight of the monster the spirit of the winds was stricken with terror. "Out and alas! We are undone!" he cried, the tears streaming down his cheeks. "Who can withstand such a being as this?"

But Ishtar remained undaunted. "Never fear," she replied gently, "for he has more brawn than brain. Though his strength be as the strength of ten, he can yet be brought low. Did we not go to school and learn from our master Ea that ancient rhyme:

> If the rock should bear and breed,
> What but stone could be its seed?
> And is there aught, now tell and say,
> So dumb as stone, so dull as clay?

It needs no hero to best him. Though you are a man, and I am but a woman, I will go and do so!"

And with these words she stripped off her garments and took in her hands tabret and cymbals and went down to the shore of the sea and made sweet music and sang.

At the sound of her music and song the sea was thrown into a wild unrest, and all the billows surged and swelled. All of a sudden there rose from the deep a huge wave, and as it rolled and broke with a mighty, resounding roar, Ishtar thought that she could hear, amid the foaming of the waters, the words of a mocking jingle repeated over and over again:

> "Deaf as well as dumb is stone,
>   Cannot hear sweet music's tone;
>   Deaf and dumb, and blind no less,
>   Cannot see your loveliness!"

Then she knew that all her efforts were in vain and that neither the magic of song nor the allure of beauty could subdue the monster. Crestfallen, she rejoined her brothers upon the crag of the mountain, and with heavy hearts the three of them made their way back to the courts of heaven.

No sooner had they arrived than the spirit of the winds at once convoked the seventy gods and ordered them to make preparations for combat. "Such war shall be waged," he cried, "as never was seen in heaven or earth! Let the storms be released from their prison, and let the tempests be unleashed! Go unto the holy mountain where the herds of God are at pasture, and bring hither the bull named Dayspring and the bull named Dusk. Yoke them to my chariot, that I may ride in fury against yon upstart!"

When the gods had obeyed these commands and all was

in readiness, the spirit of the winds mounted his chariot and lashed forth into the fray.

Meanwhile his consort Hebat sat with her maidens in the palace of heaven, awaiting the outcome of the battle. Suddenly the ground rocked beneath their feet, and there was a succession of loud knocks, as if someone were hammering under the floor. Then she knew that the monster had not been stayed but had already grown so tall as to threaten the foundations of her dwelling.

Fleeing in terror to the topmost tower, the goddess summoned her minister Takiti and bade him go down into the field of combat and bring back word concerning the fate of the spirit of the winds. But even as Takiti set out the giant frame of the monster stood athwart his path, barring his passage and blocking his vision.

Long and fierce was the struggle, but at last all the storms and tempests and all the weapons of heaven had been spent, and still the monster could not be moved. Then the spirit of the winds turned to his comrade Tasmisu and bade him go up upon a high tower and cry across the vault of heaven that all was lost and that naught was now left but surrender.

So Tasmisu went up to a high tower and called in a loud voice, "We are undone, we are undone!" And when the sound of his crying reached the ears of Hebat she grew limp and swooned and would verily have fallen from the rampart, had not her minister caught her in his arms and stayed her.

It is darkest before dawn. Now, when doom seemed to stare them in the face, Tasmisu turned all at once to the spirit of the winds, who was standing beside him.

"Brother," said he softly, "ere we go down in defeat, let us go to the city of Abzuwa * and seek the counsel of Ea, the lord of wisdom and cunning. Perchance he will search his ancient books and find a means to save us!"

So the spirit of the winds withdrew from the combat, and the two of them proceeded in all haste to the city of Abzuwa and sought the counsel of the lord of wisdom.

Now Ea is ever kind and gracious, and no sooner had he heard his suppliants' plea than he went forthwith to Nippur, to the dwelling of Enlil, and entreated his aid.

"Enlil," said he, bowing low before him, "behold, Kumarbi has created a monster to threaten the spirit of the winds and to regain the dominion of heaven by force. This monster has he planted in the waters, and minute by minute it grows taller and taller, until even now it is rocking the foundations of heaven. 'Twere best that you came to our aid, for who knows but that Kumarbi will hereafter do to you what he is now doing to us, and dispossess you from your dwelling in Nippur?"

Thereupon Enlil bethought him of the strange creature which the faery maidens had placed erewhile upon his knees, and he knew that this must be the monster of whom his suppliant was speaking; and he was loth to engage him in battle.

"Nay," cried he, "such a monster can none withstand!"

So Ea went down himself to the depths of the sea, to the place of Upelluri, the giant who holds up the sky.

"Upelluri," he cried, "know you not, and has no one told you, that Kumarbi has plotted rebellion against the king of the gods and has planted in the sea a monster made of stone,

---

* In the Sumerian language, the word *abzu* means "ocean," and it was there that the god Ea was believed to dwell. The Hittites, however, took the term to be the name of a city. It is as if they spoke of "Ea of Atlantic City" instead of "Ea of the Atlantic"!

which minute by minute grows taller and taller, until even now it is rocking Queen Hebat from her palace? Are you so remote, so far away, that you know not what passes in the rest of the world?"

But the giant merely shook his head. "No good talking to *me*," he replied. "Just write me down for a numskull. Why, even when heaven and earth were being piled upon me, I didn't notice a thing! And when later they took the magic knife and severed the one from the other, I had no idea what was happening! All I know at this moment is that my right shoulder aches. As for that monster of yours, why, I haven't even heard tell of him!"

"Stupid old man," thought Ea, and, grasping him roughly, he twisted his right shoulder and showed him the monster perched like a pillar upon it.

But the mind of Ea is shrewd and alert and swift to seize upon the slightest hint. "Magic knife, magic knife," he muttered to himself, and, again and again, "Magic knife, magic knife."

Then, as fast as his legs could carry him, he raced to the courts of heaven and called together all of the older gods— those same gods who had been present on the day when the sky was severed from the earth.

"Venerable lords," he cried, "I have found a way of deliverance. Go now and stand before the treasuries of heaven and repeat the ancient runes at which their doors fly open; for these runes are known to you only!"

So the gods went down and stood before the treasuries of heaven and recited the ancient runes, and at once the great doors swung open.

In less time than it takes to tell, Ea had entered the secret chamber, and in a few moments out he came, carrying in his hand the magic knife which in the beginning had severed heaven from earth.

Then he returned to Upelluri and stood behind his back and took the knife and cut off the feet of the monster so that it toppled from the shoulder of the giant and fell with a resounding crash into the depths of the sea. And the spirit of the winds and all his hosts gathered around it in triumph and broke it in pieces like a potter's vessel.

Thus the rebellion of Kumarbi was crushed, and the spirit of the winds reigned as lord in heaven. And from that day it has been known in heaven and earth that the race is not to the swift nor the battle to the strong.

Comment

This story is one of many dealing with the exploits of Kumarbi, chief god of the Hurrians—that is, the Horites of the Old Testament. It was adopted by the Hittites when they overran that people, and it is in a Hittite version that it has come down to us. The Hurrians themselves, however, seem to have borrowed it from the Sumerians, the most ancient known inhabitants of Babylonia, for the primeval gods Alalu and Anu, who are first introduced and the latter of whom plays a cardinal role, were gods of the Sumerians, not of the Hurrians; while a major part of the action takes place in the Sumerian city of Nippur, seat of the god Enlil, who himself also appears in the cast. The Hurrians, of course, adapted the time-honored tale to their own culture, just as do all peoples who borrow legends—or even local jokes—from their neighbors.

The central theme of the story is the creation by Kumarbi of the gigantic stone monster, Ullikummi. That creatures can be conceived of stone or rock is a commonplace of popular lore in several parts of the world (T 544.1).[1] There are, for instance, quite a number of North Caucasian folk tales based on this theme;[2] while the Arab tribe of the Beni Ṣahr, in Moab, fancifully derive their name from the belief that their ultimate ancestor was a ṣahr, or rock;[3] and the Paressi Indians of Matto Grosso assert that the first man, a certain Darukavaitere, was made of stone, being born of a stone mother named Maiso. Readers of the classics will at once recall the myth of Deucalion and Pyrrha, which relates how the world was repeopled after the Flood from stones which those two survivors cast behind their backs; and virtually the same story is found also among the Macusi of Guiana (A 1245.1). There is an interesting survival of the belief in a famous passage of the *Odyssey* (xix, 163), where Penelope says to Odysseus:

> Say whence thou art, for not of fabulous birth
> Art thou, nor from the oak *nor from the rock*.[4]

And a further echo of it may be heard in the familiar words of the prophet Jeremiah (2:27): "The house of Israel is ashamed . . . which say to a stock, Thou art my father; and to a stone, Thou hast brought me forth."

---

[1] Cf. Max Semper, *Rassen und Religionen im alten Vorderasien* (Heidelberg: C. Winter, 1930), pp. 179–86; William Francis Jackson Knight, *Cumaean Gates* (Oxford: B. Blackwell, 1936), pp. 9 ff.; J. Layard, *Stone Men of Malekula* (London: Chatto & Windus, 1942).

[2] Cf. A. von Löwis of Menar, *Archiv für Religionswissenschaft,* vol. xiii (1910), pp. 509–24; xiv (1911), pp. 641 ff.; xv (1912), p. 305.

[3] Joseph A. Jaussen, *Coutumes des arabes au pays de Moab* (Paris: V. Lecoffre, 1908), p. 107.

[4] From the translation by William Cowper.

But the stone monster of our story was no mere robot, like the creature in Capek's play or like the golem in the familiar Jewish legend. He was not created—as might appear at first glance—simply to provide an invincible champion for his father. His primary function was to shoot up like a pillar, growing taller by the minute, and eventually to rock the foundations of heaven, thus sending his father's foes toppling from their thrones and scampering for shelter. Only as an afterthought was he instructed subsequently to assume the role of a warrior and make sure that the ousted gods were given no chance to re-establish themselves in an earthly city. It is essential to his character and function, and not simply a flight of poetic fancy, that he could not be defeated even though all the winds and storms were unleashed against him; only when he was severed from the giant who supported him did he—literally—meet his downfall.

Like all the other stories in this book, this one too incorporates several bits of popular lore which would have been familiar enough to its original hearers but which need to be explained to a modern reader. We shall take them up in the order of their appearance.

First, then, there is the idea that the primeval gods reigned each for nine years. This is based on the ancient notion that an eight- or nine-year spell constituted a single "lease of life," at the end of which the order of things had to be renewed. Homer tells us, for example, that each incarnation of Minos, the "perpetual" king of Crete, reigned for nine seasons, and that nine seasons comprised the life of the two giants, Otos and Ephialtes, who sought to scale heaven and were put to death. In the *Odyssey*, Circe's enchanted victims are likened to "nine-year old swine," while the poet Hesiod describes an old ox as "one who has lived

---

[5] Cf. Gilbert Murray, *The Rise of the Greek Epic* (London: H. Milford, 1907), p. 127.

through nine seasons." [5] Spartan kings held tenure for eight years and were replaced in the ninth; while in more modern cultures— as, for instance, in Calicut on the Malabar coast—a similar twelve-year system often prevails. The Biblical "seven fat years" and "seven lean years" of Pharaoh's dream belong, of course, to the same general sphere of ideas, as does also the institution, among the ancient Hebrews, of the "seventh year of release," when the land lay fallow, and slaves were set free. In the same way, too, the ancient week often consisted of nine days. This is mentioned frequently in the *Iliad* and *Odyssey,* and it was the common practice in Rome [6]—a practice which survives in the Catholic novena and in the popular expression, "a nine days' wonder."

The next point of interest is the amusing impregnation of the male Kumarbi. One portion of the divine seed which he swallows is subsequently ejected and falls upon Mount Kanzura, where the incident arouses consternation among the gods. The remainder, however, develops into two children, one of whom is eventually delivered from his loins. A close parallel to this is afforded by the familiar Greek myth, relating how Dionysus was born from the thigh of Zeus; while an ancient Indian legend tells how the hero Yuvanāsva drank a potion intended for his wife and thereby gave birth to a son from his side. The motif appears also in a number of European and African folk tales (T 541.5).

The circumstances of the delivery are described with rare humor. To read the tale as a formal and solemn "theogony" is to miss the fun. The imprisoned embryos have no natural means of egress, and the gods are at sixes and sevens trying to persuade them to emerge from the various orifices of Kumarbi's body. Each time the embryos protest ironically that this would be "un-

[6] Cf. T. W. Allen, W. R. Halliday, and E. E. Sikes, *The Homeric Hymns,* second edition (Oxford: Clarendon Press, 1936), p. 125.

natural" and might impair them! Finally he is forced to submit to what can best be described as a primitive Caesarean section; Ea, the god of wisdom and science, cuts a "window" in his side, but only one of the monsters comes forth. Then, in desperation, the "pregnant" father tries to procure an abortion by swallowing a drug—a motif which recurs in the Greek myth of Metis (T 572.2.2)—but the drug merely gives him a toothache! Later the other monster is mysteriously delivered "from his loins."

As soon as the child is delivered, a number of guests assemble to recite incantations over it and to celebrate a sacrifice or feast. Exactly the same thing is described in various ancient Babylonian texts which relate how, at the moment of birth, Ea calls upon all classes of society to perform various rites designed to avert attacks by the child-stealing vampire Lamashtu.[7] Something very similar occurs also in modern Arab usage. On the seventh day after a birth female friends of the mother forgather in her house to carry out various magical ceremonies. A brass mortar is struck with a pestle in order to scare away the demons; the child is shaken in a sieve and is carried through the women's quarters while candles are borne before it. In the evening the father gives a feast for his friends.[8] In the same way, too, it is common practice among the Mandaeans of Iraq, and likewise among the Bogos of Abyssinia and in West African Togoland, for friends of the mother, or local priests, to ring handbells at the moment of delivery as a means of forfending demons.

Even more dramatic are the events which attended the birth of the stone monster.

First, the child is placed on his father's knees. This, in ancient times, was a common method of acknowledging paternity, the knees being regarded as seats of the seminal fluid. Indeed, the

---

[7] Cf. Bruno Meissner, *Babylonien und Assyrien* (Heidelberg: C. Winter, 1925), vol. ii, pp. 224 f.

[8] Cf. E. W. Lane, *An Account of the Manners and Customs of the Modern Egyptians* (London: C. Knight & Co., 1846), Chapter XXVII.

very word "knee" (Latin, *genu*) is connected etymologically with the words "genus" and "generation," and the term "genuine" meant originally one who has been acknowledged upon his father's knees.[9]

Second, the child is given the name Ullikummi because, as his father declares, he is destined to lay waste the city of Kummi. This method of naming an infant after some crucial utterance of its father or mother is familiar from the Old Testament; all the sons of Jacob, for instance, are named on this principle.[10] Similarly, an ancient Egyptian story fancifully derives the names of the first three kings of the Fifth Dynasty from words uttered by their father at the time of their birth; [11] while Rabelais tells us that Gargantua was so called because, when the child demanded drink as soon as he was born, his father exclaimed, *"Que grand tu as"* (*le gousier*)—i.e., What a huge gullet you have!

Lastly, the monster is placed on the right shoulder of Upelluri, a giant who lives in the subterranean ocean and supports the combined weight of earth and heaven. Such a figure is known to the folklore of many peoples (A 842). The most familiar example is, of course, the Greek Atlas, of whom Homer says that he lived in the heart of the ocean and supported not only the sky but also the earth. Similarly, the Chichba Indians of Colombia believe that the world rests on the shoulders of a giant named Chibchachum, while the Tlingits and various Athapascan tribes assert that it is held in place by Hayicanako, the Old Woman Beneath Us.

The fact that Kumarbi bids the faery maidens place the monster on the *right* shoulder of the giant is more significant than might appear at first sight. "The habit of carrying the chil-

---

[9] Cf. A. Meillet, *Bulletin de la Société de Linguistique,* vol. xxvii (1926), pp. 54 ff.; W. Déonna, *Revue archéologique,* vol. i (1939), pp. 224–35; R. B. Onians, *The Origins of European Thought about the Body, the Mind, etc.,* second edition (1951), pp. 174 ff.; J. Grimm, *Deutsche Reichsaltertümer* (Göttingen: In der Dieterichschen Buchhandlung, 1899), p. 598.

[10] Cf. Genesis 29–30.

[11] G. Lefebvre, *Romans et contes égyptiens de l'époque pharaonique* (1949), pp. 87 ff.

dren on the shoulders," says a modern Syrian-American writer,[12] "is, I believe, unknown to the West, but is universal in the East. In early infancy the little ones are carried in the arms. . . . As soon, however, as the child is old enough to sit up alone, it is carried on the shoulder. The mother lifts the child and places it astride her right shoulder, and instinctively the little one clings to her head." To be sure, in the present story the child actually stands on the giant's shoulder, for he is eventually detached from it by having his feet cut off. The general idea seems, however, to be the same: the faery maidens [13] are simply the counterparts of earthly nurses, and Kumarbi's plan is to get them to place the babe on the right shoulder of Upelluri in the belief that they are merely handing it to him to "mind." (When he speaks of its growing so tall that it will eventually touch the sky, they naturally take his words to be no more than a pious wish for the child's healthy development.)

The prodigious growth of a child born miraculously is likewise a commonplace of popular lore. The same legend was told by the Babylonians concerning their national god, Marduk (see p. 69); the Greeks told it of both Heracles and Dionysus, and the Jews of Moses; while it is also found among the Chinese, the Philippines, and various North American tribes (T 615).

The episode in which the goddess Ishtar attempts to appease the monster by music and song introduces a favorite motif of ancient Near Eastern storytellers. Another Hittite myth tells virtually the same tale in describing how the goddess sought to assuage a mighty dragon named Hedammu, while an Egyptian papyrus of the Eighteenth or Nineteenth Dynasty (1550–1200 B.C.) relates that the Canaanite Astarte once tried the same tactics on the lord of the sea when he was oppressing the hosts of

[12] Abraham Mitrio Rihbany, *The Syrian Christ* (Boston: Houghton Mifflin Co., 1916), pp. 389 ff.

[13] In the original text they are called the Irshirra-goddesses, about whom nothing further is known. "Faery maidens" is simply an approximation.

heaven. There is, however, more to the idea than the mere be-
guiling of the senses by pleasant sounds. To the primitive, "music
hath charms" in a very real sense, for it is everywhere regarded as
an effective method of breaking spells; and world folklore is full
of the story of the magic song or tune which can move mountains
and set all nature dancing (D 1275.1). The most obvious example is, of course, the Greek legend of Orpheus:

> Orpheus with his lute made trees
> And the mountain tops that freeze
>   Bow themselves when he did sing:
> To his music plants and flowers
> Ever sprung, as suns and showers
>   There had made a lasting spring.
>
> Every thing that heard him play,
> Even the billows of the sea,
>   Hung their heads, and then lay by.[14]

Similarly, a Russian folk tale tells of a merchant named Sedko
who played the harp on the shore of Lake Ilmen and so agitated
the waters that, on the third day, the king of the lake emerged and
offered him untold riches; while in the Finnish Kalevala the god
Wäinämöinen plays the harp so beautifully that all nature, and
even the king of the sea, listens entranced:

> Ahto, king of all the billows,
> Grass-beard ancient of the waters,
> Mounted to the water's surface,
> Climbed upon a water-lily,
> To the notes with joy he listened,
> And he spoke the words which follow:
> "Never have I heard such music
> In the course of all my lifetime,

---

[14] Shakespeare, *King Henry the Eighth,* Act III, Scene 1.

As is played by Wäinämöinen,
Joyous and primeval minstrel." [15]

And at the strains of Wipunen's song the water stands still.

Lastly we come to the dénouement of the tale. Here there are three items of popular lore which invite attention.

The first is the tacit assumption that a giant is necessarily a numskull: Upelluri does not even know that he is carrying the stone monster on his shoulder, and although he supports the combined weight of heaven and earth, when the one was primevally sundered from the other he "didn't feel a thing." This conception of the stupid giant or ogre is universal. In Old Norse, for instance, the word *dumbr* which really means "dunderheads," is often used as a synonym for "giants," and in later German folklore giants are commonly called *dumme Lutten* or *Lubbe*—i.e., "lubbers." Similarly, the Hebrew name for Orion, the giant huntsman, really means "Fool"; while stories of the stupid ogre who is bested by trickery form a regular category of folk tales among all peoples, no less than two hundred variations on this theme having thus far been recorded.[16]

Second, there is the element of the magic runes which are credited with the power of opening the treasuries of heaven. This, of course, is a variation of the familiar "Open Sesame" motif, which is widespread throughout the world (D 1552.2; N 455.3). The original text says expressly that it was "the ancient gods" who were called upon to recite the formula. At first sight, this might seem to imply no more than "the time-honored, venerable gods." Actually, however, there is a special point in the words: only the older generation of gods, who existed already in primeval times, would be conversant with the magic runes.

[15] Rune xli (W. F. Kirby's translation).
[16] Cf. A. Aarne and S. Thompson, *The Types of the Folk-Tale* (Helsinki: Suomalainen tiedeakatemia, Academia scientiarum fennica, 1928), Nos. 1000–1199; cf. also G 501 in Thompson's *Motif-Index*.

Third, there is the magic knife which primordially severed heaven from earth. Although there is nowhere else any direct mention of the knife, the idea that heaven and earth were forcibly sundered is by no means uncommon. Thus, a Maori tale relates that in early times the cruel forest-god Tutenganahau violently separated his parents, the sky-god Rangi and the earth-goddess Papa, who lay joined together, and parallels to this may be found in such diverse cultures as those of the Aztecs, the Indonesians, and the Samoans (A 625.2). It has even been suggested that the opening verse of the Bible ("In the beginning God created the heaven and the earth") contains a reminiscence of this idea, for the Hebrew word which is rendered "created" may originally have meant "sundered."

The initial portion of this story (up to the defeat of Kumarbi, p. 115) was published in 1936 by Emil Forrer. The rest has been subsequently pieced together from more than forty clay tablets by H. G. Güterbock, H. Otten, and E. Laroche. Fragments of a Hurrian (Horite) version are reported to have been found at Boghazköy, but they have not yet been published.

In view of the poor condition of the tablets, a few passages have here been reconstructed or elaborated on a purely imaginative basis. Thus, the encounter between Anu and the youthful spirit of the wind (p. 114), and likewise the conversation between Kumarbi and the lord of the sea concerning the creation of the stone monster (p. 116), both of which are essential ingredients of the tale, have been supplied freely from the sequel; while the incident of the child's stretching forth its hand and accidentally smashing the vase (p. 117) has been assumed in order to give point to Kumarbi's subsequent utterance. Lastly, the gist and substance of Ishtar's speech of encouragement to the sun-god and Tasmisu (p. 119) have been reconstructed from a few fragmentary phrases.

8

THE SNARING

OF THE DRAGON

I

Once upon a time the god of the winds and the dragon of the deep fell into a violent quarrel, each insisting that he was mightier than the other. At length they came to blows, and the dragon got the better of his rival, beating him black and blue.

His body sore and his pride offended, the god of the winds determined to turn the tables on the dragon by means of a trick: he would invite him to a banquet and make him drunk; then he could easily overcome him. He therefore summoned the goddess Inaras and ordered her to prepare a sumptuous feast, at which not only the gods but also the monster would be his guests.

Inaras did as she was ordered, and presently tables were spread with all manner of tasty foods and with brimming bowls of wine and drink.

At the same time, however, she decided of her own accord to improve on the storm-god's plan and to make the success of it doubly sure. "For," thought she, "suppose the dragon does *not* get drunk; then all of the gods will be at his mercy, and they will be but courting disaster if they try to overcome him. Better that a mortal should risk his neck than that any of the gods should come to grief."

She therefore went to the city of men and, meeting a man named Hupasiyas, implored him to come to the banquet and engage the dragon.

Hupasiyas, however, was no less afraid of the monster than was the goddess herself, for he knew full well that where even the strongest of the gods had failed a mere mortal could scarcely hope to succeed, unless he were somehow provided with more than human strength.

Now according to the belief of ancient peoples, there was one sure way in which such strength could be obtained, and that was if a man embraced a goddess, for with her love a goddess gave also something of her godhead. Hupasiyas therefore made the condition that Inaras should grant him this favor, and she readily agreed.

Then, after she had fulfilled her promise, she led him to the scene of the banquet and hid him out of sight.

When all was in readiness Inaras put on her finest clothes and went in person to invite the dragon.

The monster needed no coaxing, for dragons are greedy creatures and can never resist a meal. Up he came from his lair, with all his attendants around him, and presently he was sitting beside the gods, emptying the platters of meat and draining the bowls of wine. But the more he guzzled and the more he gulped, the more his body began to swell, until at last he was well nigh bursting out of his skin. Then, when he could eat and drink no more, he rose unsteadily from the table and lumbered off home. But when he got there he found that he had grown so fat and sleek that, however much he wriggled and writhed and however much he twisted and turned, he could not manage to creep back into his hole!

This was the moment for which both the storm-god and Inaras had been waiting. In less time than it takes to tell, out sprang Hupasiyas from his hiding and promptly bound the dragon with a rope; and it was then but a simple matter for the storm-god to arrive and finish him off.

For Inaras, however, the end of the dragon was the beginning of trouble. Suddenly a terrible thought flashed across her mind: if Hupasiyas were now to return home, he would certainly pass on to his wife the divine power which he had himself received. She, in turn, would pass it on to her children, and in time there would arise a family of men equal to the gods. That, thought Inaras, must be stopped at all costs. She therefore built a house on a high, unapproachable cliff and placed Hupasiyas within it, beyond the reach of humankind.

One day, however, it happened that the goddess had to go out of doors in order to do an errand. Fearing that Hupasiyas might grow lonesome and homesick and try to run away, she told him especially not to look out of the window. "For if you do," said she, "you will see your wife and children, and the sight of them will fill you with longing."

For twenty days Hupasiyas obeyed the command. But when the goddess did not return he grew both restless and bold, and at last, when he could endure it no longer, he pushed open the window and looked out. Sure enough, there in the valley below were his wife and children, and as soon as he saw them he was overwhelmed with longing.

THE SLAYING OF THE DRAGON ILLUYANKAS

Rock sculpture from Malatia; c. 1500 B.C.

In due course Inaras came back from her errand. Scarcely, however, had she set foot in the house, when Hupasiyas started to wheedle and whine, begging her to let him go home.

The goddess noticed that the window was open and realized at once what had happened. Scolding him roundly, she told him never to open it again. But even as she spoke she knew that her words were in vain; for Hupasiyas was now so far gone with longing that she could no longer hope to hold him, and it was certain that the next time she left the house he would promptly make his escape.

There was now but one thing left to do, if the godly power was to be kept from men. Upbraiding him loudly for his disobedience, the goddess put the mortal to death and set the house afire.

Through the open window came the winds of the storm-god to fan the flames.

II

The god of the storm and the dragon of the deep were old and bitter foes, for each believed that he was mightier and stronger than the other. If the storm-god huffed and puffed with his winds, the dragon roared and raged with his waves; and if the storm-god sent thunder and rain, the dragon countered with swell and squall.

One day their quarrel became especially fierce, and they fell to pounding and mauling each other until, in the end, the dragon succeeded in plucking out the heart and eyes of his rival. This, of course, did not cause him to die, for—unlike human beings—gods can live without their hearts;

but it certainly dealt the storm-god a grievous blow and left him good for nothing.

For a long time the storm-god nursed his wounds and thought up plans for besting the dragon and getting back what the monster had stolen. At last the opportunity came.

He went down to earth, and married the daughter of a humble peasant. In due course she bore him a son.

When the lad grew up, with whom should he fall in love but the daughter of the dragon? To the maiden, of course, he was simply a mortal man; neither she nor her family suspected whose son he was. To the storm-god, however, this was the golden chance, and as soon as he heard about the matter he resolved to turn it to his own advantage.

"Son," said he, "soon you will be going to the maiden's house to sue for her hand in marriage. When her father asks you what you would like as a wedding gift, say that you would like the heart and eyes of the storm-god!"

The lad did as he was bidden, and when he went to sue for the maiden and they inquired of him what he wanted as a gift, he first asked for the heart and then for the eyes. Both were readily given him, and he returned home and handed them to his father.

In a short while the storm-god had fully recovered his strength, and down he went to the sea to do battle with the dragon. Fuming and flashing and blowing and blasting, he succeeded this time in laying him low.

It so happened, however, that while the battle was raging the storm-god's son was being entertained in his future father-in-law's house. When he heard the clamor and saw the dragon sink, he knew to his dismay that he had been used as a dupe and deluded by his own father into the supreme crime of betraying his host. Honor and ancient tradition demanded that he make atonement for this offense. He therefore called to his father, aloft in the heavens, "Father, include me too! Have no mercy on me!"

The storm-god took him at his word and, coming with flail and flash, slew both the dragon and his own son.

He who would exploit others in the end pays the price himself.

Comment

Every year, when the rains were about to return and the rivers were in danger of overflowing, the ancient Hittites held a festival which they called Puruli. Part of the ceremony of that festival was the recital of the story of the snaring of the dragon. The underlying purpose of the story was to relate how in the past the terrible dragon of the swollen rivers had indeed been curbed; and, in line with universal popular belief, it was held that if the story be but duly related—or, better still, enacted—the same result would again ensue.

Such recitals and performances are worldwide. As late as 1903, for example, it was still customary at Ufford, Suffolk, in England, to parade the effigy of the defeated dragon during Rogationtide; while at Ragusa, in Sicily, an enormous dragon, complete with movable tail and eyes, was likewise borne in procession on Saint George's Day, April 23. A sixteenth-century chronicle from the English city of Leicester records an annual disbursement of municipal funds for the purpose of "dryssing the dragon"; while in the counties of Kent and Derbyshire the Feast of Saint George is still characterized by the performance of a mummers' play dealing with the defeat of the dragon at the hands of England's patron saint. At Fuerth, in Bavaria, the slaying of the dragon is enacted annually on the Sunday following Corpus Christi; and at Rouen it is asserted that Saint Romanus delivered that city from the Dragon Gargouille on Ascension Day.

The conception of a river as a dragon or serpent is, of course, universal. We shall meet it again in the Canaanite "Story of Baal" presented elsewhere in this volume (pp. 209 ff.); while in Greek myth Deianeira of Calydon was said to have been wooed by the river Achelous in the form of a snake. Among the Arabs waterspouts are regarded as dragons, and in Switzerland a mountain torrent is called a *drach* (serpent). Similarly in Chinese folklore, when an overflowing river is confined, it is said that "the dragon has been caged."

This seasonal myth later lost its specific setting and entered the domain of literature as a story of the primeval struggle between order and chaos and as a presage of the great battle to be fought by God at the end of the present dispensation. The Bible, for example, alludes frequently (e.g., Isaiah 51:9; Psalm 74:14; Psalm 89:10; Job 26:12) to the primordial contest between Jehovah and the dragon Leviathan or Rahab ("Rager"); and both the prophet Isaiah (27:1) and the Book of Revelation (12) take this struggle as the model of what will occur again at the end of days. Similarly Babylonian myth recounts the combat between the high god and a dragon named Labbu; Indic myth that between Indra and Vritra; and Greek myth that between Zeus and Typhon.

The Hittites told the story in two ways. In the one version the central theme was the greed and gullibility of the dragon—qualities which are attributed to the monster in the folklore of all peoples (G 582; G 520–26). In the other, it was the obligation of a guest toward his host.

The first version introduces a motif that needs to be explained. Before the mortal Hupasiyas will engage the dragon he insists that the goddess Inaras must consort with him and thereby impart to him something of her own divine essence. Later, when the monster has been defeated, the goddess in turn insists that Hupasiyas be spirited away to an inaccessible cliff and never again see his wife and kin. The underlying idea is that qualities can be transmitted from one person to another through kissing, embracing, or other forms of intimate contact. The idea is widespread. Often the qualities which are thought to be thus transmitted are weakness and debility. Odysseus, it will be remembered, refused to yield to Circe's advances on the grounds that his vigor would be impaired; while the Zulus of our own day assert that if a man falls in battle it is because his wife's "lap is unlucky." Similarly, in parts of South Africa a man, when in bed, may not touch his wife with his right hand, for if he did so he would have no strength in war and would surely be slain. Indeed, it is a not uncommon theme of folk tales that the very sight of a woman can render a man weak (C 312). Sometimes, however, the idea works the other way, and the qualities which are acquired are those of extra strength and power.[1] This is the case in our story; Hupasiyas insists on acquiring divine power before he will undertake to fight the dragon, but once this power has been given the goddess is equally insistent that he shall part company with his wife, lest he in turn transmit it to her and it become the property of mankind!

The same idea reappears in the familiar story in Chapter 6 of

[1] Examples are presented in the writer's *Thespis* (New York: 1950), pp. 327 ff.

the Book of Genesis. The "sons of God" consort with the daughters of men, and God therefore curtails the life of man, on the grounds that "My spirit shall not continue in man forever." In other words, he cannot tolerate the thought that human flesh may thereby have acquired the quality of the divine.

9

KESSI

THE HUNTSMAN

Once upon a time there was a huntsman named Kessi. His father was dead, and he lived alone with his mother, whom he loved dearly. Every morning he would rise up early and set out for the hills, and every evening he would come back, bringing choice venison for her supper. Moreover, so skillful was he in the chase that even the gods came to depend on him for their daily food, for every night when he returned home he would place upon their altars a portion of what he had caught.

But one day everything changed; for Kessi fell in love with a beautiful maiden named Shintalimeni, the youngest of seven sisters, and no sooner had he won her and made her his bride than all thought of hunting went clean out of his head, and he sat at home the livelong day, gazing into her eyes or listening to the tinkling music that fell from her lips.

When his mother saw what was happening she was greatly put out and began to chide and upbraid him. "Kessi," said she, "once you were the mightiest huntsman in the land— none so daring and none so brave. But look at you now; you are yourself ensnared! While the gods go hungry and your mother starves, all you do is to sit at home, mooning over a pretty wench!"

At these words Kessi was stung to the quick, and in less time than it takes to tell he had grasped his spear and called up his hounds and was off once more upon the chase.

But if a man forgets the gods the gods forget him, and when Kessi reached the hills all the beasts had gone into hiding, and however much he hunted and stalked there was no reward for his pains. For three months he wandered and roamed, ashamed to go home empty-handed and hoping against hope that his luck would turn. At last, footsore and weary, he sank down beneath a shady tree and fell asleep.

Now it so happened that the place where he lay was one of the favorite haunts of the trolls—those mischievous mountain folk whose chief delight is to plague and torment mortals. As soon as they caught sight of him and saw that he had trespassed upon their domain, they began to flock around him, dancing and tripping and capering and gamboling, minded to gobble him up.

But it is not only trolls that live in the mountains. There too dwell the spirits of the dead; and all the time that the trolls were gathering around his son, Kessi's father was watching from the top of the hill and bethinking himself how he might save him. All of a sudden an idea struck him.

"Trolls," he cried—and his voice sounded like the rumbling of thunder—"why bother to gobble him up? He will learn his lesson just the same if you but steal his cloak. For then he will shiver and freeze and soon go rushing off home to warm himself beside the fire!"

Now trolls are thievish fellows, and Kessi's father knew full well that nothing pleases them more than a chance to steal. "Yes, yes," they cried eagerly, scarce able to repress their glee. "We will steal his cloak!" And straightway they forgot altogether about gobbling him up and began to tug and pull at his cloak until they had ripped it from him and were carrying it off in triumph to their dens.

When Kessi awoke the sun had set, and the wind had turned, and a dank evening mist was rising from the ground. Instinctively he reached out his hand to gather his cloak around him, but it was gone! Anxiously Kessi groped for it in the lush grass, and all the while the wind grew colder and sharper and whistled about him and whipped his back like a lash, and the hounds barked and bayed at the cold, unsmiling moon.

At last, bowing his head to the gathering storm, he turned and picked his steps down the mountainside in the direction of a solitary light which blinked and glimmered in the valley below. . . .

A few nights later Kessi had a number of strange dreams. He seemed to be standing before a huge door, trying desperately to open it; but for all his efforts it remained closed. Then he was in the back yard of a house, where the handmaids were busy at their chores, when all at once a gigantic bird swooped down from the sky and carried one of them off. Then, again, he was looking out upon a wide open field. In the distance there was a small cluster of men who seemed to be strolling leisurely across it. Suddenly there was a blinding flash, and a fiery bolt came hurtling from heaven and fell squarely upon them. Then too the scene changed, and a throng of Kessi's ancestors were revealed, standing around a fire, busily fanning it into a blaze.

Nor were these the only visions that came to disturb him. In yet another dream Kessi saw himself with his hands bound and his feet shackled in chains such as women wear for adornment. And then he beheld himself setting forth on the chase, but as he left the house he encountered on one side of the door a crouching dragon, and on the other hideous and horrendous harpies.

At sunrise Kessi awoke and at once related the dreams to his mother. "Mother," said he, "these dreams can mean but one thing. If ever again I take to the hills the trolls will come and gobble me up! What am I to do?"

"Never fear," replied his mother calmly. "Remember the old song:

> Tall rushes bow beneath the wind and rain,
> Yet, in a moment, lift their heads again.
>
> When rivers rise, and floods o'erwhelm the land,
> Strong cities tremble, yet anon they stand.
>
> Ofttimes men cry in panic, 'Lo, we die!'
> They cried before—and yet are here to cry!

Set no store by idle dreams. Take once more to the hills, for naught will befall you!"

Then she fumbled in the folds of her robe and at length drew forth a skein of blue wool. "Take this," she said, kissing him on the cheek, "and carry it with you, for there is high magic in it, and it will protect you from hurt and harm." So Kessi set forth once more to hunt upon the hills.

Here ends the portion of the story which has come down to us. The rest is a reconstruction, the grounds for which are explained in the commentary following the story.

But the gods were still angry at the way he had neglected them, and they caused all the beasts to flee into hiding.

For a long while Kessi wandered and roamed, hoping against hope that his luck would turn. Then, when he was at the end of his strength and about to give up in despair, a strange thing happened. All of a sudden he found himself in front of a huge door. On one side of it crouched a dragon, and on the other stood hideous and horrendous harpies.

For several minutes Kessi stood staring in amazement. Then, very timidly, he tiptoed toward it and tried the latch. But the door was locked. His curiosity rising by the minute, Kessi hammered and banged. But there was no reply. At last, worn out with the effort, he sat down and waited. "Someone," thought he, "is sure to come along and let me in."

It was a long wait, and gradually tiredness overcame him and he fell asleep. When he awoke it was growing dark, and the long shadows were beginning to steal across the hills. Kessi rose to his feet and shook himself and made ready to return home. But all at once there appeared in the distance a small, glimmering light, moving steadily toward him. Nearer and nearer it came, and brighter and brighter it grew, until Kessi was all but blinded by the glare and put his hands before his eyes. When he removed them, there, standing before him, was a tall, radiant figure, clothed in light, and in his hand he held a gleaming key.

"Stranger," said Kessi, bowing before him, "I have waited long before this door and am weary and forespent. I pray you, let me in."

But the stranger shook his head. "Nay," said he, "that can I not do. For this is the door of the sunset, and beyond it lies the realm of the dead. No mortal who passes through it can ever come back."

At these words Kessi was dumfounded.

"How, then," he stammered, staring at the key which the stranger held in his hand, "how, then, can you pass through?"

The stranger smiled. "I," said he, "am the sun." And, turning the key in the lock, he passed within.

Meanwhile, on the other side of the door the spirits of the departed were gathering together to welcome the arrival of the sun-god on his nightly visit; and among them was Udipsharri, the father of Kessi's beautiful bride.

When he heard his son-in-law's voice he was overjoyed. "Never before," thought he, "have the living come to visit the dead. Now, at long last, I shall be able to hear of my loved ones."

No sooner, therefore, had the door opened than he pressed forward to the head of the throng and, falling at the feet of the sun-god, began to entreat him.

"Good master," he cried, the tears welling in his eyes, "grant that Kessi may pass through the door, for I would hear news of my kinsmen."

"Nay," replied the sun-god sternly. "That may be granted to no man except he die. Only the gods may pass through the door."

But Udipsharri would not be stayed and continued to plead and implore.

"Very well," said the sun-god at last, "let Kessi pass within and let him follow my steps down the dark path. But once he has entered these realms he may never return to the land of the living. Keep him under guard and let him not out of your sight. Bind his hands and hobble his feet, and yourself walk at his side, lest perchance he turn and seek to escape. When he has seen all things and reached the end of the path, deliver him over to me, for then I shall put him to death."

Scarcely were the words out of his mouth than the great door swung open again and Kessi found himself at the entrance of a long and narrow tunnel. A few yards ahead the figure of the sun-god could be dimly discerned, moving slowly into the distance, his bright light growing smaller and smaller until it seemed no more than a pinpoint.

At once Udipsharri stepped forward and bound Kessi's hands and put chains upon his feet. Then he beckoned to Kessi to follow, at his side, in the wake of the receding gleam.

On and on they walked, and while Kessi shuffled along under the constraint of the chains Udipsharri kept plying him with questions about the fate and fortune of his loved ones in the world of the living. Suddenly, as they rounded a bend in the tunnel, Kessi stopped short; for there, in a kind of clearing, was the very scene which he had beheld in his dream. Silhouetted against a red glow were hundreds upon hundreds of departed spirits, standing around a fire, fanning it with gigantic bellows.

"Who are these?" he whispered to his companion.

"These," replied Udipsharri, "are the craftsmen of God who forge the thunderbolts and the lightning which he hurls upon the earth."

A few paces farther Kessi halted again, for now there echoed through the darkness a loud and persistent whirring of wings, as if a thousand birds were fluttering about him; and presently he felt something soft and cold and damp brush against his cheek. He turned aghast to his companion.

But Udipsharri had read his thoughts. "These," said he, "are the birds of death, which carry the souls of the departed to the world below."

And even as he spoke it seemed to Kessi that he could discern through the gloom the shape of the giant bird he had seen in his dream.

Suddenly the little light which had been moving steadily ahead moved no more, and as they drew near and the full radiance shone upon them Kessi saw that they had come to the end of the tunnel; and there was the sun-god, standing in front of a massive door, a strange smile playing about his lips.

"Kessi," said he, "you have reached the gate of the sunrise, and farther you may not go. The time has come for you to die; for beyond lies the land of the living, and thither you may never return."

When he heard these words Kessi was filled with trembling, and he bowed himself low to the ground and clutched the hem of the sun-god's robe.

"Lord God," he cried, and his voice was choked with tears, "take me not in the noontide of my days, for I would see my beloved once more ere my time comes!"

Then the sun-god was moved to pity, and he remembered how aforetime Kessi had walked faithfully before him and provendered him daily at the peril of his life. Gently he raised him to his feet.

"Kessi," he said, and all the mercy of heaven was in his tones, "he that has seen the things of death may nevermore return to the land of the living. Howbeit, I will take you to a world of light, you and your bride also, for I will set you amid the stars forever."

On a cloudless night you may see the Huntsman standing in heaven, and beside him, a sevenfold glory, are Shintali-meni and her six sisters. But the hands of the Huntsman are bound, and about his feet are chains such as women wear for adornment.

Comment

This story is an intriguing puzzle. All that we have of it is the opening portion of the Hittite original and the small and tantalizing fragment of an Akkadian version found over fifty years ago at Tell el Amarna, in Egypt. The problem is to reconstruct the rest. This I have tried to do on the basis of several clues afforded by the part which has survived. Those clues are as follows:

1. Kessi has a series of dreams, each of which involves something which is commonly associated in popular lore with death or the realm of the dead.

(a) *There is a door that will not open.* In the Hittite version this is not further described, but in the Akkadian fragment there is again mention of a door, and there it is somehow connected with the sun-god, and the story apparently says that while mortals cannot enter the door, gods can. Accordingly, there can be little doubt that the door in question is that of the subterranean tunnel through which the sun was believed to pass nightly into the world of the dead. We have already met with it in "The Adventures of Gilgamesh" (p. 36). The door is, of course, ultimately identical with the gate of Hades which is a commonplace of all descriptions of the Descent into the Netherworld (e.g., Vergil, *Aeneid,* vi, 127). It is frequently located on a mountain knoll (F 91), so that when Kessi again took to the hills he could easily have come upon it.

(b) *A bird swoops down from the sky and carries off a hand-maid from her work.* Birds were commonly regarded as the transporters of the dead to the netherworld. There is an echo of this idea in "The Adventures of Gilgamesh" (p. 34), and it appears also both in Iranian and Finno-Ugric mythology.[1]

(c) *Kessi's "divine fathers" are seen fanning a fire.* The "divine fathers" are simply deceased ancestors, for when a king or nobleman died the Hittites said, "He has become a god." What is here envisaged is the familiar picture of the fire of hell, or perhaps more specifically that of the forge of the thunderbolts which was usually located in a mountain and thought to be manned by dwarfs or similar demonic beings (compare the myth of the Cyclopean forge on Mount Etna, which is simply a variation on the same theme).

(d) *At the door of Kessi's house—so he dreams—stand a dragon and certain female creatures called the Damnassara-goddesses.* These latter are mentioned in other Hittite texts, and in one they seem to be described as having the quality of gorgons.[2] What we have, therefore, is a dream-transference of the common notion that the entrance to the underworld is guarded by monsters. This too recurs in the story of Gilgamesh (p. 36), while Vergil says expressly (*Aeneid*, vi, 285–89) that gorgons, harpies, and similar grisly creatures stood at the gateway of Hades.

(e) *Kessi dreams that a fiery bolt comes hurtling from heaven and falls squarely upon a number of persons.* In the story of Gilgamesh, Enkidu has a similar dream which portends approaching death.

---

[1] A. J. Carnoy, *The Mythology of All Races,* vol. vi, *Iranian Mythology* (Boston: M. Jones & Co., 1917), p. 144; U. Holmberg, *Finno-Ugric Mythology* (Boston: Archaeological Institute of America, Marshall Jones Co., 1927), pp. 10–11.

[2] E. Forrer, in *Palestine Exploration Quarterly* (1937), pp. 109 f.

Now everyone who has ever heard a folk tale knows that whenever there is question of a dream the rest of the story deals with how the dream was fulfilled, and that there must always be the closest correspondence between the subsequent adventures and what has been foreseen. Accordingly, since all of the things that Kessi saw could have been readily reproduced in the netherworld, it seems pretty obvious that the rest of our story must have described his journey to that region. This means that he must once again have set out for the mountain, for it is only in the mountain that he could have found the door to Hades. And here our second clue comes in.

2. When Kessi relates the dreams to his mother, she bids him be of good heart and indeed venture again upon the hills. Then there is mention of a skein of blue wool which, apparently, she hands him. Now the fact is that in the Near East, as well as in several other parts of the world, blue is a favorite apotropaic color—that is, it is thought to avert demons and similar harmful beings.[3] The Israelites, for example, were commanded to put a cord of blue on the fringe of their garments (Numbers 15:38), and it is now generally agreed among scholars that this was originally a form of protective amulet. Hence, what is presumed by this otherwise inexplicable—not to say irrelevant—incident is that Kessi had to be protected against the perils of some new adventure in which he indeed engaged; and it implies further that the adventure in question involved an encounter with harmful beings who were thereby rendered innocuous. Either, therefore, the provision of the blue wool was a precaution against further assault by the trolls or, like the golden bough with which Aeneas was required to equip himself, it was a means of protection against the evil spirits (i.e., the guardian monsters) of the netherworld.

3. The Akkadian fragment introduces Kessi's father-in-law

---

[3] See: Hugo Gressmann, *Palästinas Erdgeruch* (Berlin: K. Curtius, 1909), pp. 8 f.; Ellen C. Sykes, *Persia and Its People* (London: Methuen & Co., Ltd., 1910), p. 336; *Handwörterbuch des deutschen Aberglaubens*, vol. i, pp. 1376 ff.

Udipsharri in connection with his arrival at the barred door. The natural inference is that Udipsharri was one of the host of spirits which crowded around the entrance to the netherworld at the approach of the living mortal. The obvious parallel is Odysseus's encounter with his mother, or that of Aeneas with his father Anchises, in similar circumstances. Dante's meeting with Beatrice belongs, of course, within the same general sphere of ideas. Moreover, since the reference to Udipsharri seems to occur in a speech by the sun-god, it seems fair to assume that the father-in-law somehow intervened with that deity to grant access to Kessi. From this it is, in turn, no great step to infer that Kessi might have been committed to Udipsharri's charge during the perilous journey and that Udipsharri might thus have acted as escort, playing the same role as did the Cumaean Sibyl to Aeneas or Vergil to Dante.

On the basis of these clues, then, I have assumed that Kessi's dreams were fulfilled by his returning to the mountain on his mother's advice, there coming upon the door of the netherworld, and, after being admitted through it, journeying through the darkling regions and witnessing, in unexpected contexts, the several things he had seen in his dreams.

But, since it is against all the laws of fact, faith, and folklore for a man to go down to Hades and return, there must have been something in the story which provided an alternative fate for the hero; and when we begin to wonder what this could have been, three further clues come to our rescue.

First, Kessi is a huntsman. Second, one of his dreams is that he is chained and fettered, and this, like the others, is a presage of what awaits him. Third, his bride's name is *Shinta*limeni,[4] and in the Hurrian (Horite) language, to which that name belongs, the word *shint-* means "seven." Combine these hints, and the alluring possibility emerges that Kessi was really none other than Orion;

---

[4] A variant has "Shintamini."

for (a) Orion was a huntsman; (b) he was chained to the sky; and (c) he was represented as pursuing the seven sisters—especially the youngest of them—who subsequently became the Pleiades.

If this identification is correct, the required end of our story is at once supplied: unable to return to the world of men, the huntsman was translated to the stars, and because he longed for his bride she too was translated with him, along with her sisters—even as one may see with his own eyes on a clear and cloudless night.

This story too contains several details of popular lore which have to be explained if it is to become fully intelligible.

Perhaps the most interesting feature from this point of view is the reference to the trolls who live in the mountains and attempt to harass Kessi on his first expedition thither; for this would appear to be the earliest mention of such creatures in any literature. The original text speaks of them simply as "junior gods" or as "sons of the gods," but there can be little doubt that what is meant is the congregation of typical mountain-sprites, more especially since demons and similar harmful beings were commonly styled "sons (or spawn) of God" by the Babylonians and Assyrians. Moreover, what makes this identification even more plausible is the subsequent allusion (fragmentary and enigmatic, to be sure) to the removal of Kessi's cloak, for this would chime in with the universal idea that trolls are given essentially to thieving (F 451.5.2.2; F 451.5.2.7). Anyone who consults Thomas Keightley's famous *Fairy Mythology* will find a score of entertaining tales revolving around this theme.

Scarcely less arresting is the manifest allusion to the idea that the ancestral dead inhabit the hills (E 481.3). All that is actually said in the original is that Kessi's "divine father" addressed the trolls from the top of the mountain, but it is only upon the assumption that this widespread belief likewise obtained among the tellers of the story that the incident becomes clear. To the original hearers of the tale this would have been common knowledge, taken for granted.

Lastly, there are the dreams. The seven [5] dreams of Kessi are probably to be regarded as a standard list of portents on which ancient storytellers drew whenever their narratives demanded such an incident. Some of them bear a remarkable similarity to one or another of the twelve dreams of Senachi in the Persian *Kalila wa-Dimna* and the Syriac *Gate of Belar*—famous adaptations of the great Sanskrit collection of stories, the *Panchatantra*. Thus, Senachi's eighth dream is of fire falling from heaven; his eleventh, of men wearing chaplets or bands; and his twelfth, of grisly semihuman creatures with terrible eyes, matted hair, long legs, and nails like the claws of vultures.

The original says that when he woke up Kessi "proceeded to relate the dreams of the night to his mother." Her reply, however, is contained in lines which have been but imperfectly preserved. First, there is reference to grass which grows up. Then there is mention of "a city," followed by the words "furthermore a river flows down apace." Next comes an allusion to the woodland or forest, and then something about "panic" and about someone's saying, "We are going to die." Lastly there occur the significant words "behold . . . blue [wo]ol." Now since Kessi's mother does not specify the same objects as were seen by him in his dream, it is plain that she is not giving an interpretation of them, as might at first be supposed. What she is doing is to reassure him, so that he will not be deterred from going out again upon the mountains; and it is, indeed, to protect him upon that venture that she finally hands him the skein of blue wool (see p. 154). Hence the general sense must have been something like this: "Grass grows tall; the wind blows upon it and bows it; neverthe-

---

[5] The description of the first dream is broken away on the clay tablet.

less, when the wind has passed, it again stands erect. A city stands beside a river; the river overflows, and it seems as though the city will be destroyed; nevertheless, when the flood ebbs the city remains standing. A hurricane rages for a day in the forest; nevertheless, the forest survives. Sudden panic besets mankind, and men say, 'We are going to die'; nevertheless, they live on. So it is with your dreams; they may disturb you for a moment, but you should not be overcome by them. Go again upon the chase and take with you as an amulet this skein of blue wool." Because her speech would thus consist in a string of proverbial sayings, I have assumed that she chanted a familiar jingle, and have therefore translated it as verse.

10

MASTER GOOD
AND MASTER BAD

*There is an old saying that a rotten apple spoils
the one which lies next to it. The same is true of
men: the bad do harm to the good.
And thereby hangs a tale.*

It all happened a long, long time ago in the city of Shudul,
which lies far away in the land of Lulluwa. In that city lived
a man named Appu. He was a rich and prosperous man; his
flocks and herds abounded over the countryside, and his gold
and treasures were heaped high as haystacks. But although
he was blessed with riches and with worldly goods, he had
no son, and this made him very unhappy. Time and again
the elders of the city would gather together at a banquet, and
each would sit with his son beside him, while poor Appu was
left to sit all alone.

For a long while he nursed his sorrow in secret, burying it
deep within his heart so that no one knew anything about it.
But at last he could bear it no longer. So one morning, as
soon as the sun was up, he rose and made his way to the
temple of the gods and laid his anguish squarely before them
and entreated their grace.

"Go back home," replied the gods, "and sleep with your wife. Then you will surely have a son."

Now Appu was a simple soul, and no sooner did he hear these words than he rushed home as fast as his legs could carry him and, without even stopping to take off his boots, jumped into bed and called for his wife.

When Mrs. Appu saw this strange behavior she was greatly amazed. But she knew what to do. At once she sent for the handmaids and questioned them one by one.

"Tell me," she inquired, "has he ever been taken like this with *you?*"

"Certainly not!" they each replied, scarce repressing a giggle.

Thereupon, without further ado, she went in to Appu and lay down beside him, fully clothed.

"What has come over you?" she demanded. "What is the meaning of this?"

But Appu would brook no questions. "Silence!" he replied brusquely. "Do as you are told! Women know nothing of these things!" And with these words he turned over on his side and went to sleep.

Well, morning came, and simple-minded Appu awoke eagerly, looked, then rubbed his eyes and looked again. But there was no child!

"Something is wrong," said he to himself. "This is not what the gods promised."

So he rose and took a snow-white lamb and made his way to the temple of the sun-god to complain before him and seek his advice. But even before he had reached his goal the sun-god looked down from heaven and saw him plodding along, a glum look on his face. So all at once the god changed

himself into a handsome youth, and presently he was standing before Appu on the highway.

"Good morrow," he said kindly, as Appu drew near.
"What brings you so early to the temple? Tell me your
trouble, and maybe I can cure it."

Appu smiled wanly. "Friend," he replied, "mine is a
trouble which no mortal can cure; for the gods have deceived
me. Only yesterday they told me distinctly that if I slept
with my wife I would have a son. Well, I did; but when I
woke up this morning there was no son to be seen!"

At these words the sun-god chuckled softly, and a merry
twinkle came into his eyes. "Nay, sir," said he. "That may
soon be cured. Go home once more, and tonight lie down
with your wife and embrace her and enjoy her. Then you will
surely get a son."

So Appu retraced his steps, while the sun-god went back
to heaven to entreat the favor of God upon the hapless and
foolish mortal.

But as soon as God saw him approaching he was seized
with alarm, and at once he sent for his vizier.

"Look," he cried, "the sun-god is rushing toward us. What
brings him hither in such haste? Maybe there is something
amiss upon earth—some disaster has befallen men's cities,
or a war has broken out!"

Regardless of his fears, however, he ordered the visitor to
be welcomed with food and drink and to be ushered into his
presence. Then the sun-god bowed low before God and explained that he had come on behalf of Appu.

"Very well," said God, when he had heard the plea, "Appu
shall indeed have a son."

Meanwhile Appu had reached home. All the way he had

been turning over in his mind what the stranger had told him. "Maybe," thought he, "he knows more about these things than the gods."

So when night fell he retired to his couch and lay down beside his wife and embraced and enjoyed her.

Well, sure enough, before the season had come around again Appu was the father of a bouncing boy. At once the midwife came and placed the child on his lap. "Sir," said she, "you must give him a name."

Appu dandled the baby up and down and fondled it and caressed it, and all the while he was racking his brain to find a name. At length he broke out into a broad smile.

"I have it!" he exclaimed. "The perfect name! I shall call him Bad."

"Why Bad?" asked the midwife.

"Simple," replied the numskull blandly. "Before I got him the gods played me a bad trick!"

Now, blessings do not come singly, and, lo and behold, within a matter of minutes the child had a twin brother. Once again along came the midwife and placed it on Appu's lap. "Sir," said she, "you must give him a name."

And once again Appu dandled the baby up and down and fondled it and caressed it, and all the while he was racking his brain to find a name. At length he broke out into a broad smile.

"I have it!" he exclaimed. "The perfect name! I shall call him Good."

"Why Good?" asked the midwife.

"Simple," replied the numskull blandly. "*Now* the gods have done me a good turn!"

Well, the lads grew up, and by the time they had reached manhood both their father and their mother had gone to their rest, leaving the property to the sons. One day Master Bad came to his brother with a proposal. "Brother," said he, "why should we stay together any longer? Let us go our separate ways, and each set up for himself!"

Master Good was taken by surprise. "Why should we do that?" he inquired, scarce believing his ears.

"Because," replied his brother calmly, "it is the way of the world. Remember the old song:

> Tho' mountains form a single chain,
> By valleys are they cleft in twain.
> Tho' rivers all run to the sea,
> Each its course runs separately.
> Tho' gods one kindred are, they dwell
> Each in his own citadel!"

When he heard the words of the familiar rhyme, Master Good was at once persuaded, and soon the two brothers were busily dividing the property between them. Presently they came to the cattle, and this was the moment for which Master Bad had been waiting.

"This for me," he said boldly, taking the sleekest cow for himself. "And that for you." And he pointed to the leanest and waved his hand gaily and made ready to depart.

"Not so fast!" cried his brother, quivering with rage. "Share and share alike! Are we not twins?"

"First come, first served!" retorted Master Bad. "Am I not the elder? And what says the law? 'The larger portion to the eldest, the smaller to the others.'"

Master Good was now beside himself with anger. "Trickster and cheat!" he shouted. "You shall pay for this! Let us go to the palace of justice and ask the sun-god to decide!"

"As you wish," replied his brother proudly. "But it will do you no good. The law is the law."

So off they went to the palace of justice and placed the matter before the sun-god.

The sun-god listened to them gravely. Then he stroked his beard. "In my opinion," he pronounced at length, "Brother Good has been defrauded, and amends must be made."

"Defrauded?" screamed Master Bad. "What about the law? The law says clearly that the eldest is to have the most, and I refuse to give up the cow. If Brother Good does not like it, let him take the matter to a higher court and appeal to the queen of heaven!" And with these words he flounced out of the palace.

The sun-god said nothing, but a mischievous, knowing smile played around the corners of his mouth.

Well, as I told you, the cow which Master Good had acquired was a lean and hungry creature; and one day the sun-god looked down from heaven, and what was his surprise when he found that she had well nigh eaten up the whole meadow!

"Mistress Cow," said he, "why do you never stop nibbling? Soon there will be nothing left!"

"My lord," replied the cow in a mournful voice, "you can see for yourself how skinny I am. I am trying to make myself sleek so that I may be of some use to my master."

At these words the sun-god was moved to pity. "Never fear," said he gently, "for a wondrous thing is about to happen, and you shall yet outshine all of your kind." And therewith he came down in all his power, and the cow was bathed in a glorious light, and all of a sudden—she was heavy with young.

Nine months later her time came upon her, and when at last she gave birth, no calf was it that she cast but *a human child*.

As soon as she set eyes upon him she was filled with alarm, and presently the air was rent with her anguished cries. "Alas! Alas!" she lowed, frantic with grief and amazement. "What a monster have I brought forth! Look, it has but two legs!" And she tossed her head like an angry wave and charged like a lion to gobble the child up.

But at that moment the sun-god came down from heaven, and his glare dazzled her eyes so that she could no longer see before her, and at last she fled in dismay. Then the sun-god provided green shoots for the child to eat, and the brooks and rivulets washed him clean.

Days passed, and when the sun-god again looked down from heaven and saw the child lying helpless in the meadow, he called at once to his servant and bade him descend to the earth and place the child on the ledge of a rock.

"Let no harm befall him," he commanded. "If eagle or vulture swoop down upon him, let the stormwinds blow and break their wings! And let no serpent dare attack him!"

So the servant of the sun-god went down to the earth and took the child and placed him on the ledge of a rock.

Now it so happened that beside the rock there was a stream, and in the stream there was a man, fishing. He had come there early in the morning and had left his basket on the ledge while he waded into the waters. At last, when the shadows were beginning to lengthen and when he was making ready to go home, he chanced to raise his eyes toward the rock, and there, caught in the gleam of the setting sun, was a strange, unfamiliar object, which seemed to move. With eager steps the fisherman raced to the spot, and, lo and behold, in place of the basket he had expected to find, there lay a baby boy, wriggling on the hard stone and sobbing.

In a moment the kindly man had caught up the infant in his arms. "How often," said he to himself as he dandled him upon his knee, "have I prayed in my heart that someday a miracle like this would happen, and the sun-god would exchange my basket for a son and heir! Now at last he has answered my prayer!" And, clasping the child to his bosom, he no longer troubled to retrieve the basket. "Never mind about the victuals." He sighed. "The Lord knows what fare is best for his creatures!"

Tenderly and with carefully chosen steps he carried the child back to his home in the city of Urma. When he arrived he was dead tired and sank wearily into a chair and called his wife and showed her the child.

"Listen closely," he said. "Take this child, and go into the inner chamber and lie down upon the bed and start screaming. The whole city will hear you, and at once everyone will say, 'The fisherman's wife is having a child,' and come hurrying hither with food and provisions. Now do exactly as I say, however odd it may seem. Woman's wit may be shrewd enough, but there are times when it needs guidance; and even if the gods have given her a good head she can still make use of a husband's advice!"

So the woman did as he told her and took the child and

went into the inner chamber and lay down upon the bed and began to scream. And, sure enough, the whole city heard her, and at once everyone said, "The fisherman's wife is having a child," and came running to the house, bearing presents of food and provisions.

The rest of the story has not come down to us. But who can doubt that the child who had come into the world so strangely grew up to be the leader and hero of his people and came back at last, after many adventures, to avenge Master Good upon his wicked and greedy brother?

Comment

This story is a combination of comedy and adventure. Appu is a typical "literal numskull," a favorite subject of folk tale and jest throughout the world. When the gods tell him that he will get a son if he lies with his wife, he runs home and does so in the most literal and bizarre manner; and when the good lady asks him to explain his behavior he replies grandly, "Women know nothing of these things!" The next morning he is astonished that no son has appeared. Later he has to be initiated into "the facts of life" by a mere stripling—really, of course, the kindly sun-god in disguise—and when the first of the twins is born his immediate reaction is to name it "Bad" on the grounds that "before I got him the gods played me a bad trick." It takes the birth of a second child to make the poor noodle realize that his luck has changed.

Stories of the "numskull bridegroom" who carries out in too literal a manner the admonitions and advice given to him by his elders are fairly universal and have added to the gaiety of nations in all ages (J 2450–99). He is told, for instance, to be sure to put parsley in the soup, so he promptly drops into it a dog of that name. He is told to "clear the room" in preparation for the arrival of the bride; so he promptly throws out the furniture, stove and all. He is told to "cast sheep's eyes" at her; so he buys some at the butcher's and hurls them in her face!

The first part of our story is set in Shudul, described in the original as a city of the land of Lulluwa, "which lies by the sea." No such city is known from other sources, but Lulluwa is simply the country of the Lullu, an outlandish people who lived somewhere in the highlands of Armenia, in the general area of Lake Urmiah. The reference to the "sea" is not to be taken too literally. While this was—and still is—a common designation for the lake, it is more probable that it is here to be understood in the somewhat vaguer sense of a remote region, just as in medieval Hebrew tales "the province beside the sea" means simply a distant land. This extreme limit of the earth was believed, naturally enough, to be the home of exceptionally simple and untutored people—our own word "outlandish" expresses the idea to perfection. In precisely the same way, the Greeks told fantastic stories about the Cimmerians and Mossynoikoi (F 129), who likewise lived in distant, sequestered parts; while tall tales were also current concerning the inhabitants of faraway India and Ethiopia. The general implication, therefore, is something like "back of the beyond" or "Timbuctoo," real places conceived as a kind of Cockaigne or Schlauraffenland—a fitting homeland for the noodle Appu.

The idea that twins are hostile to each other is, again, a commonplace of popular lore (T 685.2). We need think only of Jacob and Esau, Set and Osiris, Romulus and Remus, and Balder and Hodr. The exact tenor of the argument between Master Bad and Master Good is not stated in the original text, which says only that the former took the good (i.e., sleek) cow for himself, and left the lean one for his brother. Since, however, they both subsequently referred the dispute to the god of justice, it is plain that some point of law was involved. Hence, as best meeting both the logical and dramatic requirements of the story, I have assumed that it turned on the question of how property should be divided when the heirs to it were twins, and that the precise course of the altercation was described in that part of the original tablet which is now broken away. This, of course, is purely a guess; unfortunately, there is no mention of inheritance in the portions of the Hittite code of laws which have come down to us, while of Hurrian law—which would have been implied, if our story came ultimately from the Hurrians—we as yet know too little.

The latter part of our story revolves around two familiar themes. The first is that savior heroes are born of animals (B 631) who themselves conceive in miraculous fashion. More specifically, the Egyptian Horus was often portrayed as born of the cow-goddess Hathor, while Egyptian pharaohs are represented as being suckled at the udders of a cow. In one of the Canaanite myths from Ras Shamra, Baal is said to mate with a cow. The implication is, therefore, that the lean and unprepossessing cow acquired by Master Good eventually attained to the highest honor reserved for any beast.

As to the miraculous form of conception—through impregnation by the sun—this finds an excellent parallel in the ancient Egyptian belief about the sacred bull, Apis. "The Apis calf," says Herodotus, "is born of a cow which never afterward is able to bear young. The Egyptians say that a blaze of sunlight comes down from heaven and strikes it, whereupon it conceives." Similar also is the Greek myth of how Zeus wooed Danae in a shower of gold— a tale which is told in substantially the same way among the Kirghiz of Siberia; while the same powers are attributed to the sun in Chinese, Samoan, and Aztec folk tales (T 521), and in many parts of the world it is considered imprudent to let a girl see the sun until she has reached the age of puberty, or even, in some cases, her thirtieth birthday (C 756.2).

The second theme is that of the Exposed Child (R 131), familiar especially from the legends of Moses, Sargon of Agade, Perseus, Oedipus, Paris, and Romulus and Remus. Lord Raglan has pointed out [1] that the tale of the child exposed or spirited away and subsequently rescued by chance is a standard element in the sagas of great gods or national heroes in all civilizations, recurring—to cite but a few instances—in the myths of Zeus, Asclepius, Apollo, Dionysus, and Jason among the Greeks, and in those of Arthur and Llew Llawgyffes among the British and Welsh respectively. Note especially that the child is often said to be exposed *beside water:* Moses, on the banks of the Nile; Sargon, of the Euphrates; and Romulus and Remus, of the Tiber.

Our story is introduced by a fragmentary sentence which seems to say that if bad men are brought into too close contact with good ones they are apt to "bruise" or damage the latter. This sentence is evidently the "moral" of the tale, and it may be suggested, in view especially of the verbs employed, that in its complete form it stated that "just as rotten apples spoil good ones, so bad men brought into too close contact with good ones, confer injury upon the latter." We should thus have a Hittite forerunner of the well-known medieval adage: *Pomum compunctum corrupuit sibi junctum.* An early English rendering may be found in *The Agenbite of Inwit* (1340): "A roten appel among the holen [whole ones] maketh rotie the yzounde [sound ones], yef [if] he is long there among." Another version occurs in Chaucer's "Cook's Tale," and a modern rendering in Fanny Hurst's *Hallelujah:* "Every rotten apple in the basket is an enemy to the rest of the apples."

This story has been put together by H. G. Güterbock [2] from two different cuneiform texts. The first extends to the point where

[1] FitzRoy Richard Somerset, Lord Raglan, *The Hero* (London: Methuen & Co., Ltd., 1936).
[2] H. G. Güterbock, *Kumarbi* (1946), pp. 119–22.

the two brothers divide their father's estate, and Master Bad takes the better portion for himself (p. 165). The rest is supplied from a second tablet, which also contains other matter. It should be observed, however, that although the two texts dovetail and form a continuity, they in fact belong to two different versions (or recensions) of the story. Indeed, some scholars [3] (among whom Güterbock himself is now, apparently, to be included) have expressed doubts as to whether, despite their apparent sequence, the two texts really form part of one and the same tale.

---

[3] See the edition by J. Friedrich in *Zeitschrift für Assyriologie*, Neue Folge, vol. xv (1950), pp. 214–33, 242–53, where the two portions are distinguished as belonging to different tales. However, Friedrich admits the possibility of a connection between them.

CANAANITE
STORIES

II

THE HEAVENLY BOW

Once upon a time there lived in the city of Haranam a king named Daniel. He was a good and worthy king, who ruled his people justly, defending the widow and protecting the orphan. But, although he had a daughter, he had no son to follow after him or to do for him those thousand and one little things which a dutiful son does for his father. At this he was very sad and one day he decided to beseech the gods to grant him the boon he craved. So he stripped off his fine robes and put on a lowly loincloth and went to the temple and served there as a scullion for seven days. Every night he would seek out a corner of the rooftop and lie down to sleep under the stars, hoping that some god would come to him in his dreams and answer his prayers.

On the seventh night his piety was rewarded. The great god Baal heard his sighing and sobbing in the darkness and carried his prayer to El, the graybearded father of the heavenly host.

"Daniel," said he, "has served us humbly as a scullion for seven days, changing his robes for a loincloth, bringing us food and drink, tending our every need. Yet his heart is heavy and sad, for he has no son. There is no one to do for him all he has done for us—no one to guard his home, none to protect his guests, none to defend his name. There is no one to launder his clothes or plaster his roof when it leaks. When he keeps festival there is no one to share his board; and when he is gay in his cups there is none on whose arm he may lean. When he dies he will die without heir, with none to preserve his name, with none to honor his shrine; and the fire on his hearth will go out. So bless him, O Father of all mankind, and grant him his prayer!"

Then El, who is ever merciful and ever kind, came down from heaven and took his servant by the hand and bade him go home and embrace his wife. "Soon," he said, "you will have a son."

At these words Daniel was overjoyed. His heart singing, his face aglow, he left the temple and made for home. And no sooner had he crossed the threshold than he summoned minstrels and dancing girls; and for seven days the house was filled with carousal, while music and song rang out like the voice of swallows in the eaves.

Eagerly and impatiently Daniel counted the months. One month, two months, three months went by, until at last, when her time was upon her, Daniel's wife gave birth to a son, and they named him Aqhat.

Several years later Daniel was sitting one day in the open treeless place which served at once as a threshing-floor and as a court of justice, when, lifting his eyes, he saw a cloud of dust in the distance. Presently, as his vision cleared, he discerned the outlines of a man coming toward him, carrying a bow and arrow. As the figure drew nearer Daniel perceived that it was indeed no man who was approaching but none other than the renowned Sir Adroit-and-Cunning, the smith and artisan of the gods, making his way from his forge in Egypt to the heavenly court on the Mountain of the North.

It was a long, long journey, and when Daniel saw that the traveler was weary and spent he at once invited him into his house.

"Hasten," he called to his wife, "and prepare a lamb for our guest, who has come from faraway Egypt!"

So a lamb was duly prepared, and wine was poured, and presently host and guest were regaling themselves at the festive board, chatting gaily together and pledging each other's health like old and trusted friends.

At last it was time to go, and the visitor rose to take his leave. But as he stood in the doorway, bidding his fond farewells, all thought of the bow and arrow went clean out of his mind, and he departed without them.

Only when he was already a long way off did Daniel notice what had happened. Then he picked up the bow and, aiming it playfully at his little son, assured him that he might have it for his own.

"But remember," he said, "the first thing you kill with it belongs to the gods."

Years passed, and Aqhat grew up into a sturdy and handsome youth. One day, while he was out hunting, a beautiful maiden suddenly appeared before him and stopped him in his tracks.

"I am the goddess Anat," she said, "and I desire your bow and arrow. If you will give them to me, I will reward you with silver and gold."

Now Anat was the goddess of warfare and the chase, and

the truth was that the bow and arrow which had been given to Aqhat were really hers, for she had ordered them from the divine smith, and it was while on his way to deliver them to her that he had stopped at Daniel's house. Aqhat, however, knew nothing of this, and did not even believe that the lovely creature who stood before him was indeed a goddess; to him she was merely a greedy girl playing a trick.

"If you want a bow," he answered brusquely, "Lebanon is full of the stuff out of which you can make one. There are trees enough for the wood, and oxen enough for the gut, and mountain-goats for the horn. And if it is really Anat who wants one, why does she come to *me?* Let her go to Sir Adroit-and-Cunning. It is *his* task, not mine, to supply weapons to the gods!"

But at these words the goddess grew only more anxious and eager. "If," said she, "you will give me the bow I will give you life everlasting. You will be like the gods and never die! You will feast every day at the table of Baal, and heavenly music will ring in your ears."

But still the youth would not yield. "Young lady," said he, "spin me no fancy tales. Such tales are but fit for children; to a grown-up man they are trash. No one on earth can escape death. Men are like clay vessels; in due time the potter pours his glaze upon them, and old age besprinkles them with fine white dust. I know full well that I too must die. Besides," he added as a parting shot, "why should you want a bow? That is a thing for men. Are the ladies taking up hunting?"

The goddess could not fail to smile at this retort. Nevertheless, she was already contriving a wily scheme. "I warn you," she replied darkly, "if you choose to tread the path of disobedience I will meet you upon it; and if you choose to walk in pride I will bring about your fall. If *you* call *me* 'young lady,' *I* can call *you* 'Prince Charming,' but that won't help things a whit, for the day will surely come when Prince Charming will be groveling at my feet!"

And with these words she made off. Speeding hotfoot to El, father of the gods, she complained to him of the youth's arrogance and insolence and demanded that he be punished. But El was a mild and gentle god and refused to interfere, regarding the whole affair as no more than a petty squabble.

At this Anat flew into a towering rage. No longer the docile daughter humbly beseeching her father, she became in a moment a fearful goddess of war, imperious, threatening, and defiant.

"Do not make fun of this," she cried. "Even without the bow, I am not unarmed. Mine is a far-reaching hand. I can come against you and smash your skull, and dye your gray locks with blood! Then you can go screaming to Aqhat and see if, for all his bows and arrows and for all his vaunted strength, he can rescue you from the hands of the goddess of war—mere maiden though she be!"

Now El was old and tired and feeble, and threats like these did not fall lightly on his ears. Frightened at his daughter's violent outburst, he attempted at once to soothe and placate her.

"Daughter," said he, "I have always known you as a gentle creature, and goddesses do not usually behave like this. Perhaps, after all, you are right. For the bow is certainly yours, and the young man has cheated you out of it. For that alone he deserves to be crushed. Do with him as you will."

Encouraged by her father's approval, Anat hastened to

carry out her scheme. Returning to Aqhat, she now posed as a spirited young girl who had run away from home.

"If," said she, "you will be a brother to me, I will be your sister, and we can go hunting together. There are wonderful grounds near the city of Abelim. Meet me there, and maybe I can teach you a few new tricks of the chase!"

Aqhat, not sensing the threatening danger, readily consented, whereupon the goddess rapidly completed her plan.

Not far from the city of Abelim lived a ruffian named Yatpan, who made a living by hiring himself out to anyone who wanted foul deeds done. Anat decided to enlist his aid and to employ him as her henchman. Gladly did Yatpan accept the charge, and at once suggested a devilish plan of attack.

"After the hunt," said he, "Aqhat will undoubtedly feel hungry and sit down in the fields to cook some of the venison for his supper. The glare of the fire will show where he is. I will follow that clue and pounce upon him."

The plan sounded simple enough, but even as the ruffian was speaking Anat felt something stirring within her, and all of a sudden she realized that she had fallen in love with the handsome prince and by no means desired his death. All she wanted now was simply and solely to recover the bow.

Brushing aside her henchman's savage proposal, she therefore laid down a milder and gentler plan. As soon, said she, as the lad sat down to his meal, vultures and other birds of prey would surely be attracted by the scent and come wheeling around. Concealing Yatpan in a sack, she herself would fly among them and, at the crucial moment, when they were directly above Aqhat's head, she would open the sack and release him. Unnoticed in the general *mêlée*, he was then to knock the breath out of the youth and, leaving him unconscious, snatch the bow and wait for her to haul him up and fly off.

In due course Aqhat indeed grew tired and hungry and sat down in the fields to cook his meal. All at once a flock of vultures came wheeling overhead, circling ever lower over their prey; and among them flew the goddess, carrying the sack in which her henchman was concealed.

Presently there was a loud whirring of wings, the sky grew black, and the air was rent with deafening shrieks, and even as the birds massed for the final swoop, the sack flew open, and out leaped Yatpan upon the hapless youth. The crucial moment had arrived; the precious bow was at last within grasp.

But now Yatpan bungled. The goddess had told him in detail what he was to do to Aqhat. She had told him to knock the breath out of his victim, meaning only that he was to render him unconscious. It so happened, however, that the words she had used could be interpreted as having a fatal meaning, and it was in this way that Yatpan chose to understand them. To that bloodthirsty ruffian they were an order to knock the breath of life out of the young prince—in other words, to beat him to death. Fiercely and relentlessly he fell to the attack, and ere many moments had passed the handsome youth lay lifeless at his feet, and the bow was safely in his hands.

When Anat saw what had happened she burst into tears. "Look what I have done!" she cried. "I have slain you, O Aqhat, for the sake of a mere bow! Would that you were still alive! Would that I could bring you back!"

But the goddess's troubles were not yet at an end, for once

again Yatpan fumbled and faltered, and this time with even more dire results. As Anat was flying him back from the scene of the assault the precious bow slipped from his hand and fell irretrievably into the sea.

Now both love and labor were entirely lost; not only had the beloved youth been slain, but the slaughter had been for nothing. And worse was still to come. For the gods had decreed of old that wherever innocent blood was shed nothing would grow. Now, therefore, the earth would languish, the crops would fail, the corn shrivel in the husk.

Meanwhile, there was King Daniel, sitting, as usual, in the open space outside the city, judging the disputes of his people and attending to the business of the realm.

Suddenly his daughter Paghat came running toward him out of the fields. "Look," she cried, "there is a flock of vultures over the house, and in the fields everything has gone dry."

What this betokened she knew full well; murder had been done, and the corpse must be lying in the fields.

At the sound of her words Daniel was seized with dismay and rent his garments in grief. "Now," he cried, "Baal will surely withhold his mercies. For seven long years there will be neither summer showers nor winter rains, and never will the searing heat be broken by welcome thunder! The grapes will wither on the vine, and the rivers run dry!"

Then he ordered his daughter to saddle an ass so that he might go and see for himself what was afoot.

Sure enough, all the crops had withered, and nothing remained in the fields save a few stray sprouts and a few solitary blades of grass.

Suddenly two of Daniel's servants were seen rushing through the meadow, their tresses flowing wild and the tears streaming down their cheeks. "Aqhat," they cried, "is dead! The goddess Anat has brought about his death!"

(The words were strangely ironic. The men had not seen the attack, and did not know that Anat had contrived it. All that they meant, for their part, was that the youth had evidently fallen while hunting and that the goddess of the chase had thus claimed another victim.)

At these tidings Daniel was filled with consternation, for he now realized that the birds which were circling and screaming overhead must have been preying upon the corpse of his son, and that, unless he could somehow recover the remains, it would be impossible to give Aqhat decent burial. Raising his eyes to heaven, he prayed to Baal.

"Baal," he cried, "send your winds and break the wings of the vultures so that they fall at my feet. If I find in them traces of fat and bone, I shall know that these are the remains of Aqhat, and I shall take them and bury them in the depths of the earth."

Scarcely had the words escaped his lips when a mighty wind began to blow, and the vultures came hurtling down from the sky. Twice he ripped open their gizzards but found neither fat nor bone. The third time, however, the fiercest of all the flock—the mother vulture herself—fell at his feet, and now there were indeed traces of human flesh.

Reverently Daniel interred the remains of his murdered son.

Then he began to seek out the culprit, visiting each of the neighboring cities and pronouncing upon it a solemn curse, should it be harboring the guilty man. But although he in fact went to Abelim, the city nearest to the scene of the crime, the murderer was nowhere to be found.

So Daniel returned home and ordered that Aqhat be mourned for seven years. And for seven long years the courts of the palace resounded to wailing and dirge, and the voice of lamentation rang out like the plaintive cry of swallows.

At last, when the time of mourning was ended, Paghat, the sister of Aqhat, resolved to take a hand. "Aqhat," said she, "has no brother to avenge him. Howbeit, if the stars will be benign and if the gods will give me their blessing, I myself will go and track down his slayer, and when I find him I will kill him!"

Thereupon, arming herself with sword and dirk and concealing beneath her cloak the rest of a warrior's gear, she set out on her expedition.

At twilight, when the sun was setting, she turned in at the nearest encampment to find lodging for the night. But to whom should her steps lead her save to Yatpan himself— the very man (though as yet she knew it not) whom she was actually seeking!

Yatpan, enchanted by her beauty and thinking also that here was a prospective customer for his services, received her warmly and promptly invited her to drink with him. Presently, when he was well in his cups, he started to boast, as drunken people will.

"Why," he exclaimed, thumping his chest, "this hand that slew Aqhat can slay foes by the thousands!"

Now the secret was out. But Paghat was shrewd and wary. If her heart was strong as a lion, her mind was nimble as a serpent. Biding her time, she kept filling his cup, until finally he slumped in his seat, drowsy and exhausted.

Quick as a flash, the brave princess drew her sword, and in a moment the villain lay dead before her.

We do not have the rest of the story. We may imagine, however, that as soon as justice had been done the curse was removed from the earth, the rains returned, and the green things sprouted once more.

We may believe also that the murdered Aqhat, whose remains King Daniel had so reverently interred, eventually rose again, when new life came to the world. For, in the thought of ancient peoples, nothing dies forever, and burial is but a prelude to resurrection. Or, if we are more fanciful, we may suppose that he was ultimately translated to the stars, where he may still be seen on a clear night in the figure of the Heavenly Huntsman.

As for the precious bow, this too may have been recovered from the depths of the sea and carried aloft to heaven, for, although we today no longer perceive it, the wise men of the East indeed saw in a group of stars the figure of a giant bow.

Comment

Ancient peoples loved to trace in the heavens the figures of gods and heroes and mythical beasts with whom they were familiar from myth and tale. They saw, as it were, the features of Kris Kringle in the face of the moon or Bambi gamboling along the Milky Way. The sky itself was the mantle of Ishtar or the cloak of Odin, or else it was a tapestry embroidered by God with the pattern of His creation. The sun was the golden-haired Apollo or the stern, all-seeing god of justice; the moon was Artemis, queen of the night; and the rainbow was Laima's girdle or the sword of Ali or the circlet of Ormuzd. The familiar cluster of the Pleiades were the virgin companions of Artemis, pursued by Orion; and one could even find in the firmament the comely tresses of Berenice, queen of Egypt.

Now of all the stars of heaven none is more striking or more brilliant than those which today form the figure of Orion. It was therefore but natural that our remote ancestors should have tried to see in them the portrait of some especially prominent and familiar character. But they were not agreed as to who it might be, and two alternative stories grew up.

According to one, it was the Giant Huntsman—the tallest, strongest and most handsome of men, who had dared to offend the goddess of the chase and had therefore been put to death. The accounts of his offense varied. Some said that he had claimed to surpass her in the hunt; others, that he had made an attempt on her virtue or annoyed her by consorting with one of her maids. But all agreed that, whatever he may have done, it was an act of presumption, and the goddess had taken her toll. Here again, stories differed. According to some, she had sent a scorpion to bite him; according to others, she had chained him to the sky; but by far the most popular tale was that she had chased him with her hounds. And if you looked closely you would observe that there was indeed a scorpion at his heels,[1] and that his giant frame was indeed bound by a belt of stars, and that there was indeed a hound baying beside him.

The other story took as its basis a curious fact which could not be squared with the traditional tale of the Huntsman—namely, that for two entire months in the year this particular group of stars is not to be seen. Late in April it disappears from the eve-

---

[1] The constellation Scorpio rises as soon as Orion sets—i.e., follows upon its heels.

ning sky, and not until July does it re-emerge upon the morning horizon. Moreover, it vanishes, in Eastern climes, just at the moment when the summer drought is about to set in. No sooner, in fact, has it slipped out of sight than at once the rains cease, the rivers run dry, the earth languishes, and no green thing grows up. To many an ancient mind this pointed to but one conclusion: the figure which the group portrayed was none other than that of the great lord of fertility—a god like the Babylonian Tammuz or the Syrian Adonis—who was indeed believed to die or disappear each year at the onset of summer and to revive or return when the drought broke.

Gradually the two stories came to be blended together, the traits and motifs of the one being boldly but deftly grafted upon the other, until at length a new composite tale burst into flower.

Such is the Canaanite tale of "The Heavenly Bow." Shorn of embellishments and elaborations, it relates how a handsome young huntsman came by chance into possession of a wondrous bow designed for the goddess of the chase, how he brashly refused to give it up, and how he was therefore put to death. All of this is simply a version of the myth of Orion. But then our tale goes on to describe how the death of the hero caused blight upon earth and how he was eventually avenged and revived; and in this part of it we may see, albeit in attenuated fashion, the myth of the Dying and Reviving God. The purpose of the combined story was to account for the conditions which prevail *both in heaven and on earth* during the dry season.

But what of the bow? Why is it that our Canaanite story revolves around the bow, while there is nothing of this in the classical myth? And why, on the other hand, is there here no mention of the hound which plays so important a role in the classical tale? The answer is both simple and intriguing. The fact is that the peoples of the ancient Near East did not recognize in the heavens the figure of the great hound. Instead they grouped the stars differently and detected next to Orion the shape of a huge bow, which they regarded as the emblem of the goddess of the chase. Accordingly, in their story of the Heavenly Huntsman it was the bow rather than the hound which had perforce to play a prominent role! And notice how deftly they worked it in: after the huntsman had been slain the goddess did not recover the bow; *it fell into the sea*. Translate this into astral terms, and the point is immediately apparent—so long as the bow appears in heaven, all is well upon earth, but when the Huntsman "falls" so too does the bow, and then the season of drought sets in! Only when both are restored does fertility return.

It is not impossible that in some earlier and more primitive form our story was used to accompany and interpret a sacred pantomime performed at a summer festival when the Huntsman and the Bow reappeared in the sky and the new year was thought to begin. Such festivals are observed in many parts of the world, and ritual pantomimes are a common feature of them. In that case, some of the incidents of the story may have been inspired or influenced by the rites of the occasion. The elaborate burial of Aqhat, for instance, and the subsequent prolonged mourning for him may well reflect the common ancient and modern custom of burying, bewailing and eventually "resurrecting" small figurines representing the dying and reviving spirit of fertility. The Egyptians used, in this way, to bury and subsequently disinter images of Osiris, and in Asia Minor mock funerals of Attis were staged. In Rumania girls go out of the villages on the Monday before Assumption, carrying a miniature coffin in which is deposited a clay puppet called Kalojan (beautiful John).[2] He is ceremonially bewailed, buried, and, a few days later, dug up again. Similar ceremonies take place also in the Abruzzi, where the image is known as Pietro Pico (little Peter).[3] It is not difficult to imagine the added dramatic effect our

[2] Marck Beza, *Paganism in Rumanian Folklore* (London: J. M. Dent & Sons Ltd., 1928), p. 30.
[3] E. Canziani, in *Folk-Lore,* vol. xxxix (1928), p. 218.

story would have acquired if it had been recited against such a background, while, in general, the influence of ritual patterns upon literary forms may now be regarded as established. (This does not mean, of course, that our story as it now stands was simply the libretto of a pantomime. What it means is that its original pattern and the delineation of some of its incidents may have been conditioned by the circumstances in which it was then recited and by the features of a performance which it was then designed to interpret.)

Into the actual telling of the story are woven many points of popular lore and custom which demand a word of comment:

1. When Daniel serves in the temple for seven days in order to entreat the gift of a son, he is performing what is called "the rite of incubation." In ancient times persons who craved a favor of the gods, or who wished to be cured of ailments, would repair to the shrine and sleep within its precincts. Their dreams were then considered to reveal the divine intent. As a rule the suppliants dressed themselves in the humble garb of pilgrims or servants, and this is what is implied in the express statement that King Daniel so attired himself.

2. The reason why Sir Adroit-and-Cunning, the divine smith, is said to come from Egypt is that he was popularly identified with the Egyptian god Ptah, whose seat and forge were in the city of Memphis. This identification was inspired by the fact that, at the time when our story was written, a great deal of Egyptian ware was circulating in Palestine and Syria. It was therefore deemed appropriate to locate the divine smithy in that land. It was as if a modern novelist were to say that his heroine was outfitted in "Paris creations." Another source of ceramic imports at this time was Crete, and for this reason other Canaanite stories place the forge of the divine artisan on that island.

3. The idea that the shedding of innocent blood pollutes the soil

and renders it infertile recurs in the Biblical story of Cain: "Cursed art thou from the ground, which hath opened her mouth to receive thy brother's blood from thy hand; when thou tillest the ground, it shall not henceforth yield unto thee its strength" (Genesis 4:11–12). Compare also the words of Numbers 35:33—"Ye shall not pollute the land wherein ye are: for blood, it polluteth the land: and no expiation can be made for the blood that is shed therein, but by the blood of him that shed it." In the final Song of Moses it is said that God avenges His servants and makes the expiation for His bloodstained land (Deuteronomy 32:43). The same idea occurs also in Sophocles, *Oedipus Rex,* 25 ff.

It is impossible to fix precisely the scene of our story. Nobody knows for certain where the city of Haranam lay. A place of that name is mentioned twice in Egyptian literature as being located in North Syria. Similarly, we do not know the whereabouts of Abelim, the spot where Aqhat was slain.

12

THE KING WHO FORGOT

Long, long ago there reigned in the city of Hubur a high and mighty king named Keret. But, although his kingdom was large and his wealth great, he was filled with sorrow and sadness, for he had neither wife nor children nor brethren to whom he might leave them when he died. Afflictions sevenfold had fallen upon him. The bride whom he had chosen had run away on the very eve of the wedding, and all his brothers had died untimely—some in full health and some in sickness, some through plague and some through mishap; and some, again, had fallen by the sword.

The more Keret thought about these things, the sadder he became; and one day, when he could contain himself no longer, he went into an inner chamber and threw himself upon his bed and wept. Loud and bitter was his weeping, and soon his couch was bedewed with tears. At last, amid sobs and sighs, he fell asleep.

Suddenly, in his dream, the whole room was bathed in light, and there beside his bed stood God himself, king of heaven and father of men, looking down into his face with an expression of infinite tenderness and love.

"What grieves you, Keret?" he asked gently. "Why is my

beloved servant so full of tears? What is it that you wish? Maybe you are not content with your kingdom and would like to have one as wide as God's? Or maybe you desire a dominion as far-flung as heaven's? If it is wealth you crave, what do you lack? There are horses and chariots aplenty in your stables, and your servants are never so many."

"Nay," answered Keret, "it is not for these things that I weep. The riches which I desire are not riches of silver and gold but of offspring, to be my heirs. What I crave is a son who may sit upon my throne when I am dead."

"And that you shall have," replied the god. "Up, now, dry your tears, and wash yourself clean. Take a lamb, a kid, and a brace of doves. Pour out wine into a silver goblet, and honey into a golden bowl. Then go up to the tower, bestride the ramparts. Raise your hands to heaven. Set out a meal for me, and bid Baal also come down and partake of food.

"When you have done this, command that corn be taken from the granaries and wheat from the public barns, so that sufficient bread may be baked to last a full six months. Then call the people to arms. Let nobody be exempt. Let your troops be three hundred myriad strong—peasants beyond number, nobles beyond count. Let them march forth in their thousands, countless as drops of rain, innumerable as the spawn of fish upon the waters. Let bachelors lock up their houses and come forth, and breadwinners be ready to abandon their kin. Let widows go out and earn their own support. Let the sick shift for themselves, and the blind trust to luck. Even if a man be but newly betrothed, let him leave his bride as he would his cattle, for another and a stranger to possess!

"After you have mustered your troops, march for six days. At sunrise on the seventh day you will come to the land of

Udum, where reigns the mighty King Pabil. Sweep through towns and hamlets. Pillage the countryside. Bring all life to a standstill. Drive before you the woodcutter, the thresher, and the drawer of water. But when you reach the capital city steal up quietly upon it. For six days shoot no arrow and fling no stone against it. At sunrise on the seventh day, when the stallions start neighing and the asses start braying and the watchdogs start baying, King Pabil will rise from his bed and suddenly behold your troops encircling his walls. Then he will send messengers to you, saying, 'Take silver and shimmering gold, servants and scullions as many as you please, steeds and chariots from the stable. Take them, Keret, as the price of peace, and begone from my courts! Do not lay siege to Udum, for the land was given to me by God!'

"When you hear these words, send back and say, 'What need have I of silver or of shimmering gold? What need have I of servants or scullions, or of steeds and chariots, be they never so many? Give me what is not in my house! Give me the maiden Horaya, the fairest of your tribe, whose beauty is as the beauty of Anat and whose grace is as the grace of Astarte, whose eyes are like shining lapis set about with rubies. Let me bask in the gaze of her eyes. For she it is that God has appointed unto me in a dream—the father of mankind, in a vision—so that I might have offspring and heirs!' "

No sooner did Keret awake than at once he did as the god had bidden him. He washed himself clean; took a lamb, a kid, and a brace of doves; poured out wine into a silver goblet and honey into a golden bowl; went up to the tower and bestrode the ramparts; raised his hands to heaven, and set out a meal for God and for Baal. Then he commanded that bread be baked and provisions stored to last a full six months, and he mustered his army and set forth.

For two days they marched, countless as locusts upon the face of the plain. At sunrise on the third day they found themselves before the shrine of Asherat, the lady of Tyre and goddess of Sidon. When Keret saw the resplendent statue of the goddess seated upon her throne, he was moved to make a vow.

"As Asherat of Tyre lives," he cried, "and as the goddess of Sidon exists, if I gain Horaya as my bride I shall pay to this goddess twice the girl's weight in silver and thrice in gold!"

Thereupon he continued to march for three more days. At sunrise on the fourth day the army indeed arrived at the land of Udum. Obedient to the command of God, they swept through the towns and hamlets, pillaging the countryside and bringing all life to a standstill. Woodcutters, threshers, and drawers of water were driven ruthlessly before them. At last they came to the capital city. For six days they called a halt outside the walls, shooting no arrows and flinging no stones. At sunrise on the seventh day, when the stallions started neighing and the asses started braying and the watchdogs started baying, King Pabil rose from his couch and looked out, and there was Keret's army drawn up against his walls.

At once he summoned his consort. "We are besieged unawares," he cried, "and must sue for peace!"

Then he dispatched messengers to the camp of Keret to entreat him to lift the siege and depart. "Tell him," he said, "that I will give him silver and shimmering gold, servants and scullions who shall stay in his household throughout

their lives, three horses also, and chariots from my stables."
But when they came and repeated their master's offer of
silver and gold and treasure, Keret spurned their words.

"What need have I of silver?" he retorted. "And what of
shimmering gold? What need have I of servants or scullions,
or of steeds and chariots, be they never so many? Give me
what is not in my house! Give me the maiden Horaya, the
fairest of your tribe, whose beauty is as the beauty of Anat
and whose grace is as the grace of Astarte, whose eyes are
like shining lapis set about with rubies!"

So the messengers went back and repeated these words to
King Pabil.

When Pabil saw that all his entreaties were vain he made
ready to deliver the maiden, and even as she was led away to
the invader's camp all the people of Udum followed in her
wake, weeping and wailing like a cow bereft of its calf or
like yeanlings who have lost their dam. "The lady Horaya,"
they cried, "is gentle as she is fair. Never was there any that
hungered but she took him by the hand; never was there any
that thirsted but she came to his aid!"

Flushed with triumph, Keret returned home. As soon as
he re-entered his palace he made a vow to Asherat to dedi-
cate to her service any male offspring of the marriage. Then
he ordered a sumptuous banquet to be held to celebrate his
marriage with the beauteous princess. There was open house
for all; no one who approached the royal precincts was turned
away. Nor was it only mortals who were regaled; all the
companies of the gods came also to share in the rejoicing.
From the earth came Baal, and from the sky came Prince
Moon, and from the underworld came Rashaf, the lord of

the plague, and from his forge in faraway Egypt came Sir Adroit-and-Cunning, the divine artisan and smith.

When the festivities were in full swing and the wine was flowing freely, the divine guests proposed to God, the leader of them all, that he rise and offer a toast to the bride and groom. So God rose from his seat and took a goblet in his hand and chanted these words:

> "Behold, this damsel, soon or late,
> Seven sons shall bear, or eight.
> The last shall as the first one shine,
> Partly human, part divine.
>
> Behold, this damsel, soon or late,
> Seven girls shall bear, or eight.
> The last of them shall rank no less
> Than the eldest-born princess!
>
> Yon bridegroom too shall rise on high
> Above all princes 'neath the sky;
> O'er all the peoples 'neath our sway
> His fame shall be supreme for aye!"

Then the gods joined in the toast and after they had eaten and drunk their fill they departed to their dwellings.

In due course Horaya conceived and indeed bore sons and daughters. But as soon as his happiness and prosperity had returned Keret forgot the vow which he had made to Asherat and began to give himself up more and more to feasting and carousing.

For seven years the goddess bided her time. Then she grew wildly incensed. "If," said she to herself, "Keret can forget me, I can forget him. I shall no longer keep him in health. I shall do to him what was done to his brethren!"

Thereupon she summoned all her children and told them what was in her mind and charged them not to come to the aid of the impious king. With one accord the gods agreed to do as their mother bade.

One day Keret decided to spread a banquet for the lords and nobles of his realm. So he sent for Horaya and told her to dress the fattest of fatlings and to pour large flagons of wine and to invite the princes to attend.

But when they were in the midst of their revels and were gaily toasting their host, the great bronze doors of the feasting-hall suddenly swung open, and there, preceded by her chamberlains and pages, stood Queen Horaya herself in all her beauty. Slowly and majestically the little procession moved to the center of the room. Then Horaya raised her hand to command silence. An expectant hush fell upon the guests.

"My lords," she said—and her voice was like tinkling bells—" 'tis not to greet you that I am come, but to bring you tidings of woe. Yesternight it was revealed to me in a dream that within a few days our lord Keret would fall sick unto death. 'Twere better, therefore, that ye should sorrow than rejoice, that ye should weep than laugh!"

The nobles stared dumfounded. Then, silently, they rose from the tables and departed.

When they were out of hearing Horaya beckoned her eldest son to her side. "My son," said she, "your father grows sick and feeble. Go in unto him and claim the scepter from his hand, that you may be king and your bride may be queen."

Sure enough, within a few days King Keret was stricken

with a grievous sickness, and when it seemed that he was nigh unto death his sons gathered to the palace to bid him a last farewell. But while all the others were secretly waiting for the hour when they would divide his possessions among them, the youngest son, Elhau, stood beside his father's bed, wracked with grief and filled with amazement.

"Father," he cried, "how can you die? For are not kings of the seed of God? Yet behold, heaven and earth are filled with sighing. All my songs are turned to dirges, and my music to the voice of tears!"

Then he laid his hand gently upon Keret's brow. "Father," he whispered, "I am not of those who desire your death. Would that you might live forever and never see death!"

"My son," replied Keret slowly, "spare your tears; for weeping befits not a grown man. Call your youngest sister, Shetmanet, that she may be here to bewail me after I am gone. Howbeit, tell her not now that I am sick, lest the stream of her tears dry up in mid-field and her spirit be heavy-laden. Wait until sundown; then tell her only that her father is giving a banquet and desires her to come with her tabret and join the minstrels."

So away sped Elhau, taking his spear in his hand, and setting off in hot haste.

When he reached the abode of Shetmanet it was already dark, and there was his sister lighting the lamps for the evening. As he neared the threshold the rays caught the tip of his spear and revealed his presence.

The moment Shetmanet espied him she was seized with alarm. "No one," thought she, "would come at this hour except to bring tidings of disaster." So she fell upon his neck and wept.

"Is aught amiss with the king?" she gasped, her voice trembling. "Is our lord sick?"

"Nay," replied Elhau. "The king is not sick. He is giving a banquet and desires your presence."

But Shetmanet could scarce believe him and, inviting him within, she tried to loosen his tongue by plying him with wine.

At last he broke down. "Yes," he said, "it is true. Keret has been sick for some three or four months."

At these words the maiden broke out into a loud lament. Then, recovering herself, she hastened with her brother into the presence of the king.

When she entered the palace, instead of minstrels and singing women, a company of wailers confronted her, and instead of taking her place at a banquet it seemed as though she were attending a wake.

Now the life of the land was bound up with the health of the king, and when the king languished so too did the land. Eagerly and anxiously the plowmen kept lifting their eyes to heaven, waiting for the rain which might prosper their crops. But no rain fell, and soon all their provisions were exhausted—all the corn in their bins and all the oil in their jars. The whole land was smitten with blight. . . .

But God, who is ever merciful, would not suffer his servant to perish. So he called all his children together and besought them to bring relief.

First he called upon the stewards of the mansion of Baal. "Wherefore," cried he, "does no rain descend upon the earth? Open the windows and let it pour forth!"

But the gods paid no heed to his words, for they would not break faith with their mother, Asherat.

Then he besought them to revive the ailing monarch. "Who among you," he cried, "will drive out the sickness, expel the disease?"

But again the gods paid no heed to his words, for they would not break faith with their mother, Asherat.

Seven times he cried. But still there was no answer.

"Very well," said he, fixing upon them a stern and scornful glance. "Stay where you are. I will perform the cure by myself! If you will not help me, I shall use magic."

And, so saying, he took in his hands rich loam and kneaded it into the shape of a dragon. Then he summoned the divine witch Sha'taqat—"She-Who-Removes-Sickness"—and, handing the image to her, he told her to fly over cities and provinces until she reached the ailing Keret. And as he sent her forth he pronounced this spell:

"Death, thyself grow sick and frail;
But thou, O witch divine, prevail!"

So the witch flew over the towns and provinces, and when at last she reached King Keret lying upon his bed of sickness she touched his head with her wand and drove out the sickness, causing it to enter the image of the dragon. Then she washed him clean of the sweat which had been pouring from him, and she restored his appetite for food.

At once he summoned Horaya and bade her set venison before him, and after three days he was fully recovered and whole.

Now, the sons of Keret knew nothing of what had passed, and on the third day Yassib, the firstborn, came to the palace, expecting to find his father lying in death, but lo and behold, when he entered the audience chamber, there was the monarch sitting upon his throne.

Yassib rubbed his eyes in amazement. "This," thought he, "is not as it seems. Keret is really on the verge of death and is propping himself up on the throne in a last desperate effort to hold it. Now is the time to do as my mother said and to claim the scepter from his hands."

Boldly he strode forward. "Sire," cried he, "you are old and feeble, and the reins are falling from your hands. No longer can you champion the poor or defend the oppressed. No longer can you feed the widow or succor the orphan. To your kinsmen and companions you are already dead. Your only kinsman is the demon of disease, and your only companion the shadow of death. Step down, then, from the throne and let *me* be king! Commit the scepter to me, and let me reign in your stead!"

When Keret heard these words he rose from the throne and stood before his son in the full glory and might of his vigor; and behold, he was as a youth in the day of battle.

"Varlet!" he cried, his eyes ablaze with anger. "Henceforth you shall be no son of mine! May the Lord of Hell split open your head, and the Goddess of Battle rend your skull! May you fall headlong off a cliff and find your teeth in your fist!"

Here ends the portion of the story preserved on the clay tablets. What follows is supplied by conjecture.

Then Yassib knew that God was indeed with Keret, and he covered his face and fled.

One after another the younger brothers of Yassib came in unto their father to claim the scepter. But as each of them arrived, expecting to find an old and feeble man, Keret rose up from his throne and stood before him in the full glory and might of his vigor and roundly cursed him and disowned him. And even as the brethren went in severally to the presence of the king, their sisters stood without, greedily awaiting the hour when their father would die and they would divide his possessions among them.

Only Elhau and Shetmanet remained in their homes, torn with grief and wracked with sorrow. When Keret saw that they had not come in to claim the kingdom he sent for them and bade them hie to the palace.

"Elhau and Shetmanet," said he, laying his hands upon their heads and kissing them tenderly upon the mouth, "to you shall belong my kingdom and my possessions, youngest of my sons and daughters though you be. For you alone have loved me and mourned me, and in your hearts alone has there been neither greed nor covetousness. Go, therefore, in peace, and know that when I die yours shall be the scepter and the birthright."

And so it was. After many days Keret died and was gathered to his fathers; and the throne passed to Elhau, and the first of the daughters' portions to Shetmanet.

Thus, in a sense which none had foreseen, the promise of God was indeed fulfilled: the last of the sons was as the first, and the youngest of the daughters inherited the portion of the eldest. Thus too those who had sought to frustrate the purpose of God were taught that his justice is supreme, and that his will is done on earth as well as in heaven.

Comment

This story, composed at some time between 1800 and 1375 B.C.,[1] is best regarded as a saga of the same general type as the legends of Alexander the Great, Charlemagne, King Arthur, and the Cid, or as the medieval *chansons de geste*. There is, to be sure, this difference, that in the present case none of the characters is known from any other source and none of the places mentioned can be definitely located. It is therefore impossible to determine what basis of fact may underlie the tale. Except to professional historians, however, this is of little importance; for whatever such basis there may be, the treatment is typically romantic, and many of the details are supplied directly from the common storehouse of popular fiction.

To take but one example, note the systematic use of the conventional number seven. At the beginning of the story we are told that its hero, Keret, had suffered sevenfold afflictions; he marches for seven days against the land of King Pabil, and for a further seven days lays siege to its capital city. The goddess Asherat waits for seven years to see whether Keret will fulfill his vow; and when the monarch is finally punished with sickness God calls seven times on the heavenly host to effect a cure.

So too the number three is employed throughout in a purely conventional manner. It is on the third day of his march that Keret comes to the shrine of Asherat; King Pabil offers him, among other things, three horses as danegeld; for three months Keret falls sick; and it is on the third day after his miraculous

---

[1] The upper limit is fixed by the mention of horses among the danegeld offered by King Pabil, and the lower limit by the fact that the city of Ugarit, in the ruins of which the clay tablets of the story were unearthed, was destroyed by fire around 1375 B.C.

cure that his impudent son Yassib, ignorant of what has happened, comes forward to claim the throne.

The author no doubt took pride in such virtuosity and skill and in his ability to tell the story well. One is led to suspect, however, that, like any true artist, he was primarily interested in the universal human values of the tale. For if one reads it carefully, with an eye to such values, one observes that it is pervaded by two basic themes. The first is that of loyalty—more particularly of conflicting loyalties. God has promised Keret that he will have offspring and that his line will not die out. Keret, in turn, has promised the goddess Asherat that his sons will be dedicated to her. Keret violates his vow, so the goddess takes revenge by sending a mortal sickness upon him. Nevertheless, despite the slight to his consort, God cannot go back on his word. Therefore he must needs cure the recalcitrant monarch. Here is the first issue of conflicting loyalties. Another is revealed in the attitude of the heavenly family. They have pledged to their mother, Asherat, that they will stand by her and withhold their aid from Keret when she brings the well-merited punishment upon him. Accordingly, even though their lord and master, God himself, invokes them to drive out the disease, they declare a strike until he is forced to circumvent their noncompliance by a blackleg recourse to magic!

In contrast to the loyalty of the gods, but pointing up the same basic theme, is the perfidy of most of the human characters. The very first thing that we are told about Keret is that his intended bride had betrayed him by absconding on the eve of the wedding. As the original text expresses it, "His lawful wife did he not obtain, even his rightful bride. He had paid the bride-price for the woman, but she went and took her departure." And the very last thing we hear of him, in the portion of the story which has come down to us, is that his eldest son conspires against him. Moreover, Keret himself breaks his vow to Asherat and forgets her as soon as prosperity has returned; while King Pabil is so faithless to his own daughter and so abominably craven that he is willing to surrender her without a murmur for the sake of keeping his kingdom and avoiding battle with an invader! The only human characters in the whole story who show loyalty and devotion are Keret's youngest son, Elhau, and his youngest daughter, Shetmanet; and it is just because they are exceptional that they are the ones to be rewarded in the end.

The second motif which permeates the story is that of the Enigmatic or Ambiguous Prophecy (M 305): no word of the gods is uttered in vain, and their every pronouncement comes to pass, even though its meaning be misunderstood and the mode of its fulfillment therefore unexpected. This is a favorite motif in the popular lore of several peoples. An instance in point is the Jewish tale of the man who was told that he would end his days in Jerusalem; he died in the Jerusalem Chamber (M 341.3.1). Another is that of the student who received from his teachers the strange blessing, "What thou sowest thou shalt not reap"; what it really meant was that his children would not predecease him (M 306.1). A similar story of an ambiguous oracle is related by Apollodorus in connection with the entry of the Heraclids into the Peloponnesus. The gods had said that the entry should be made "at the third sowing." The heroes thought this meant the third year, and launched an expedition. But that venture ended in disaster, because what the words had really connoted was the third *generation*.

In our present story, when God attends the wedding of Keret his divine companions urge him to propose a toast. With that effusive lack of reticence which characterizes such greetings in Oriental countries, he invokes upon the bridal pair abundance of offspring, and adds, "The youngest shall get a firstborn's portion." What Keret and his guests assume is that this is merely complimentary hyperbole, as who should say, "May all your geese be swans!" But the words turned out to have a deeper meaning, for in the event the impious eldest son is cut off with the proverbial shilling, while the devoted youngest son and daughter inherit their father's estate! If we had more of the story we might find also that the same kind of "surprise fulfillment" may likewise have attended the vow which Keret made to Asherat. For it is by no means impossible that the other sons too were expelled from the dominion and fled for refuge to the shrine of the goddess, so that in the end they indeed became her devotees.

Seen in the light of its universal values, the story has something of the quality of a Greek drama. Likewise based on traditional lore—perhaps even on a remote historical event—it nevertheless transcends its material and translates it into the broadest human terms. In that sense, though it may lack the artistry of the Gilgamesh epic or the magnificence of the poem of Baal, it is nevertheless a masterpiece of no mean caliber.

Three elements of popular lore and custom which appear in the story may perhaps require a word of explanation.

1. The fact that Keret is instructed to besiege King Pabil's city by night but to attack it only at dawn (pp. 191–92) is in accordance with what has always been standard Arab convention; an assault by night is regarded as cowardly.[2] Similarly, in the Biblical Book of Judges (9:32–33), when Abimelech is advised by the governor of Shechem to crush an impending revolt in that city, he is urged to "rise now by night, thou and the people which are with thee, and lie in ambush in the field. Then, in the morning, when the sun riseth, get thee up early and make a raid upon the city, and behold he [i.e., the rebel chief] and the people which come out with him will be thine."

2. The idea that fertility fails when the king falls sick reflects one of the most widespread notions of primitive cultures, namely, that the king is not so much the ruler of his people as the embodi-

[2] See G. Jacob, *Das Leben der vorislamischen Beduinen* (1895), p. 124.

ment of their collective life and spirit. It is for that reason that among several savage tribes he is actually put to death as soon as he shows signs of growing weak and feeble, and even more commonly he is deposed or executed at the end of a fixed term—either a year or a longer period—when the life-lease of his people is thought to expire and demand renewal. (This idea is the *leitmotif* of Sir James Frazer's *The Golden Bough.*) Similarly, if a king disobeys the gods, they may take their revenge by sending a blight upon the entire land. A good illustration of this may be found in the Bible, for in II Samuel 21:1 we read: "And there was a famine in the days of David three years, year after year; and David sought the face of the Lord. And the Lord said, It is for Saul, and for his bloody house, because he put to death the Gibeonites." The prayers of the Hittite king Mursilis II (c. 1350 B.C.) likewise contain mention of a twenty-year blight caused by the sins of the royal family.

3. The manner in which Keret is cured reflects the ancient and primitive usage known technically as *envoûtement*—that is, the magical transference of a disease, malady, or misfortune from a person to an image. To be sure, the practice was—and still is—used in black as well as white magic, i.e., as a means of conveying calamity as well as of removing it. A whole series of Babylonian texts has come down to us, prescribing the creation of clay images for magical purposes. The following is typical:

Pull off a piece of clay from the ocean-bed,
Fashion thereof a black figure resembling the person you wish to cure.
Bind on his head the hair of a white goat.
Place the figure on the body of the sick person.
Recite the famous Spell of Ea.
Turn the patient's face to the west.
Then the spirit which has gazed on him will stand aside,
And the demon which has seized him will vanish.[3]

[3] R. C. Thompson, *The Devils and Evil Spirits of Babylonia* (1904), vol. ii, p. 103.

Similarly, an Assyrian letter of the time of Esarhaddon (681–68 B.C.) says:

The epidemic and the plague shall not come near the palace. . . . Disease and fever shall not come near the house of any man. We have performed various ceremonies to avert it. A clay image resembling the demonic daughter of Anu, another resembling Namtar, the lord of pestilence, and another resembling the god Latarak, and a further one made out of clay drawn from the bed of a canal and resembling a man . . . have we placed before the statue of Gula, the goddess of healing.

But what is of special interest in the present case is that the image is made—apparently—in the form of a serpent or dragon; [4] for this at once recalls the brazen serpent set up by Moses in the wilderness as a means of curing the Israelites of a plague which the late redactor of the record describes as the bite of "fiery serpents" (Numbers 21:6–9). This image, we are informed, subsequently attained the status of an idol, and it was therefore broken in pieces by the pious King Hezekiah of Judah (II Kings 18:4). Magical images of serpents have indeed been found by archaeologists in several Palestinian sites.

It should be mentioned also that the incident of Queen Horaya's intervention at the banquet and of her suggestion to Yassib that he claim his father's throne (p. 197) is supplied by a somewhat conjectural restoration, since the original tablet is broken at this point. However, the actual presence of Horaya upon the scene is clearly indicated, as is also her address to the nobles. The rest is based on the occurrence of the words "in a vision" and "thy wife" among the fragments of lines which remain.

---

[4] The original text is unfortunately damaged at this point; but immediately after the description of how God made the image there occurs twice the word "serpent" or "dragon."

13

THE STORY
OF BAAL

In the gray beginning of years, when the gods were assigned their portions, earth had as yet no lord or master. Two gods especially contended for the honor; one was Baal, lord of the air and of the rain, and the other was Yam, the dragon who ruled the waters.

Said Baal, "The earth is mine, for through my rains is it quickened."

Said Yam, "The earth is mine, for through my rivers and springs is it watered and refreshed."

Long and bitter was the debate between them, until at last they came before God and besought him to settle the matter. God thought deeply about the claims of each. Then he made up his mind and called all the gods before him.

"The earth," he declared, "belongs to Yam, for water is the first of all things." And therewith he summoned the divine artisan, Sir Adroit-and-Cunning, and bade him build a palace for Yam in token of his kingship.

But at that moment there was a stir at the back of the heavenly ranks, and a diminutive creature pushed his way forward. It was Ashtar, the youngest of the gods, a mere youth in his teens.

"Sire," cried he, prostrating himself before the throne of God, "if it please thee, let *me* be king. For am I not the spirit of the rills and runnels whereby the earth is watered in the months when Baal withholds his rains and when the rivers and lakes run dry? Is it not I who sustain it when it languishes in the summer and is near to die?"

But God merely laughed in his face. "You?" he cried, his eyes twinkling merrily. "Why, you are not even old enough to manage a wife; how much less, then, to rule the earth!" And he dismissed him from his presence.

No sooner, however, was Yam ensconced in his palace than he began to behave like a tyrant and to demand exorbitant tribute from all the gods and goddesses; even the necklaces which the ladies of heaven wore for adornment had to be surrendered to his greed. At last the gods could endure it no longer, so they held council to determine what they should do. For a long while they debated and discussed, but all were agreed that to offer battle was out of the question, for the dragon was mightier than they, and none could withstand him.

Suddenly, when all of them had lapsed into silence, the goddess Astarte rose in their midst. "Brothers and sisters," she said—and her voice was like the tinkling of cymbals—"I pray you, let me go down unto the sea and entreat the dragon with my music and my charms, for perchance I may soften his heart toward us."

When the gods had nodded their approval Astarte stripped off her garments and braided her hair and scented herself with rich perfumes and took her tabret in her hand and went forth like a minstrel maid beside the shore of the sea.

Presently, as the strains of her music were wafted to his ears, the dragon rose from the deep and gazed in wonder upon her. "Daughter of song," he cried, "what brings you hither, so carefree and gay?"

"I am Astarte," replied the goddess, "and I am come to beseech your mercy upon my brothers and sisters. Very heavy is the toll which you have laid upon them, and they can pay it no more. Perchance you will relent, that their burden may be eased."

But even as she was speaking the dragon was eying her beauty and listening entranced to the music of her lips, and all his desire was aroused. "Lady," he said, "if you will offer yourself as tribute I shall ask none other. Go, tell the gods and goddesses that if they will yield to me their sister Astarte their burden shall indeed be eased!"

So Astarte went back to the courts of heaven and related what the dragon had said.

As soon as he heard her words Baal was filled with fury and went at once to the dragon and poured contumely upon him and challenged him to open combat.

"Varlet!" he cried. "May the bludgeons of heaven smite you and strike you! May the Lord of Hell split open your head, and the Goddess of Battle your skull! May you fall headlong off a cliff to find your teeth in your fist!"

At these words the dragon rose up from his throne and summoned his two messengers and ordered them to go forth to the court of God and demand the surrender of Baal and all his allies. But when the messengers arrived there was Baal, standing beside God and ministering to him like a devoted vizier; and God was loth to deliver him into the hand of his foe.

"Nay," said he, "Baal is a gentle creature and, for all his bluster, he means no harm. And even if he were to attack your master, your master is stronger than he and has naught to fear."

Baal, however, was really by no means so meek and mild as God had described him, and scarcely had the messengers departed than at once he besought his sisters Astarte and Anat—the two great goddesses of battle—to aid him in engaging the dragon.

"Baal," replied Astarte, "it were vain to approach him in close combat, for behold, there is none that can withstand him. Were I to furbish all my spears and bring forth all my weapons, they would prove of no avail; and were we both to launch into the fray all of our might, it would but be trampled into the dust! One way only there is to subdue him and win the kingship."

With these words, she called to the divine artisan, Sir Adroit-and-Cunning, and bade him fashion for Baal two magic bludgeons which, if ever they missed their mark, would return of themselves into his hand.

"With these weapons," said she, "you will be able to attack him from afar, and in the end you will prevail, and the kingship will be yours forever!"

So the divine artisan came from his forge and brought the two bludgeons and handed them to Baal. The name of the one was Driver, and of the other, Repeller.

And Baal took the bludgeon which was named Driver and hurled it against the dragon, crying, "Driver, Driver, drive Yam from his throne, the lord of the sea from his royal seat!" But the bludgeon missed its mark, and the dragon kept on threshing the waters, unharmed.

Then Baal took the bludgeon which was named Repeller and hurled it against the dragon, crying, "Repeller, Repeller, repel Yam from his throne, the lord of the sea from his royal seat!" And this time the bludgeon reached its mark, and the crest of the dragon sagged, and his countenance drooped, and he lumbered to the shore and collapsed.

"Behold," he gasped, "I am as good as dead. Let Baal be king!"

When he heard these words Baal was so overjoyed at his own triumph that he forgot altogether about the avenging of his brothers and sisters and did not even bother to finish off the dragon. But even as he was about to depart the voice of Astarte rang out in sharp rebuke.

"For shame!" she cried. "Would you leave us all unavenged? Behold, yon monster has held us in thrall and despoiled us of all we have!"

Then Baal was filled with shame, and he smote the dragon again and again between the eyes and upon the neck, until it lay senseless at his feet.

But although this was the end of Yam's dominion, it was not the end of Baal's woes. For now a new trouble confronted him: king though he was, he had no palace, and since he had no palace none of the gods would give him obedience. Turning to his sister Anat, he begged her to intervene with God, so that God might grant him permission to uprear a mansion like that of Yam.

"But approach him not directly," he counseled. "Go first to our mother, the queen Asherat, and let *her* present my petition. For, look you, whenever a god enjoys her favor, in no time at all Sir Adroit-and-Cunning is ordered to build him a mansion and equip it in silver and gold and set before him the richest fare. Go, therefore, and entreat her grace."

But all the while that he was speaking Anat's thoughts were upon the dragon, which lay prone at her feet. When she saw that he was still alive she took her spindle and beat him roundly. Then she ripped off her long robe and drove him back into the sea, herself striding after him in triumph through the towering waves.

At length she returned to the shore and, having first fashioned costly vessels which she might offer as presents, she winged her way toward the courts of God.

Queen Asherat was sitting sedately upon her throne when suddenly she descried upon the horizon a cloud of dust, and presently the imperious figure of the young goddess was seen advancing toward her. Now Anat was a goddess of battle, and when the aged queen saw her approach she was seized with terror and began to tremble, for she feared that some trouble had arisen among the family of the gods.

"What brings you hither in such haste?" she cried. "Is something amiss in the family of heaven?"

But as the young goddess came nearer Asherat saw that she carried in her hands gifts of silver and gold, and her fears were calmed. "Come," said she, "eat and drink and tell me your wish."

Then Anat poured forth to her mother the complaint of Baal and told her how all the gods were treating him with contumely, placing dirt upon his table and proffering him goblets of filth to drink.

"Very well," replied the queen benignly, "I will do as you wish. But meanwhile we must stay the dragon, lest perchance he revive and renew his attack." And therewith she summoned Sir Adroit-and-Cunning and commanded him to fashion a large net and to imprison the monster within it.

Then she ordered her lackey, Sir Holy-and-Blessed, to caparison a colt so that she might journey to the special precinct of God; and when the lackey had done so and had seated her above the gay trappings, she set forth, with Anat and Baal following on foot.

Long and wearisome was the journey, until at last they arrived at the far horizon, where the waters which are above the earth run together with those which are beneath it, and there, on the holy Hill of the North, lay the divine abode. Leaving Baal with the lackey at the foot of the mountain, the two goddesses moved forward to the dwelling of God. But when they reached the innermost preserve Anat too was bidden to wait without, and Asherat rode on alone into the presence of her consort and prostrated himself before him.

"Sire," she cried, after he had welcomed her and regaled her, "wisdom, like life everlasting, is yours, and out of your wisdom you have brought it to pass that Baal is now our king, with none above him, our sovereign with none beside him. Howbeit, he has no palace from which to reign and in which to house his family. You yourself have to shelter his children in your own mansion, while his three beautiful wives have to find lodging with me! I beseech you, grant your consent that a house be built for him."

When he heard these words a kindly smile broke over the face of God. "Why, of course!" he exclaimed. "Wherefore should Baal not have a house? But let him build it himself!

Does he think that God is a laborer, or Asherat a handmaid, that they should go setting the bricks or carrying the hod for his lordship?"

"Nay," replied the goddess, "that will he gladly do. And once again, Lord God, have you shown your wisdom. For when once Baal dwells upon earth he will be able to see for himself how it fares and so suit his gifts to its needs. No longer will all be whim and caprice. Henceforth when he sends his rains they will fall in due season, and the snows will come at the right time!"

Then she sped to Anat and brought her the glad tidings. "Go to Baal," she cried, "and bid him send to Lebanon for its choicest cedars. Let the mountains yield their silver, and the hills their finest gold. Let gems and jewels be brought, and let the palace be built and adorned!"

So Anat in turn sped to Baal and brought him the glad tidings. And Baal sent to Lebanon for its choicest cedars, and the mountains yielded their silver, and the hills their finest gold; and gems and jewels were brought for the adornment of the palace.

When all was in readiness Baal summoned before him the divine artisan, Sir Adroit-and-Cunning. "Here is the material," he said. "Now hasten and build me a palace. Uprear it on the holy Mountain of the North, and let it fill ten thousand acres!"

But the artisan had a plan of his own. "Baal," he replied, "I will build you a palace such as you desire, and shall put a fine window in it."

"No, no!" cried Baal. "No window in my palace!"

"But, Baal," insisted the artisan, "there is a reason for what I say, and in time you will see it!"

"Never mind," replied Baal with heat. "I too have a reason. If we put a window in the palace the dragon will climb through it and carry off my wives, and I shall become the laughing-stock of all!"

The artisan shrugged his shoulders. "As you wish." He sighed. "But someday you will change your mind."

So the building was set in order, and within seven days it was almost complete. Then Baal called together all the gods and goddesses and regaled them at a sumptuous feast. But suddenly, amid the revels, a terrible thought crossed his mind.

"The dragon is not dead," said he to himself. "Maybe he will escape from the net and invade the palace, and after all I shall lose the kingdom!"

So while his guests were carousing Baal went down to the seashore, to the place where the dragon lay imprisoned in the net, and he lifted his mighty trident, the emblem of his lightnings, and smote the dragon roundly upon the skull until no breath remained within him. Then Baal wandered over the face of the earth, journeying from city to city and from province to province, taking each as his possession and proclaiming himself its king.

At last he returned to the scene of the feast and took his place in the midst of his guests and summoned the artisan to his side. "Sir Adroit," said he, "the danger is past. You may now put a window in the palace, for I have found a use for it. Whenever that window is opened it will be a sign that the earth needs rain, and at that very moment the windows of heaven will likewise be opened, and the rains will pour forth."

When he heard these words the artisan could scarcely

conceal his delight. "Sire," he replied, "that was my plan from the beginning. Did I not tell you that you would change your mind?" And therewith he broke out into the strains of an ancient hymn of praise; and this is the song he sang:

"When Baal's holy voice rings out,
When Baal's thunders peal,
    The earth doth shake,   the mountains quake,
The highlands rock and reel.

His foemen cling to mountainsides,
Or to the woodlands race;
    From east to west,   in wild unrest,
They flee before his face."

Nor, indeed, could Baal himself forbear to cap the verses which his servant intoned; and, lifting his voice, he proceeded to chime in with the closing words of the familiar hymn:

"Ye enemies of Baal, tell:
Now wherefore do ye quail?
    'Because his eye   is swift to spy,
His hand is strong to flail!

Who seeks his order to defy
Is stricken at the last;
    Strong cedars tall   do wilt and fall
Beneath his angry blast!' "

Then he paused for a moment and looked around him at the assembled gods and goddesses, and a smile of content-ment played around his lips. "Henceforth," he said, "I alone shall reign over gods and men, and neither king nor com-

moner shall dispute my right. Henceforth the earth shall be
my estate, and none shall invade it!"

But all of a sudden his expression changed, for he bethought him of his rival Mot, the terrible spirit of death and
drought, who lived in the netherworld and the desert places
and whom he had purposely excluded from the banquet.
"Maybe," he mused, "Mot is even now plotting rebellion
and planning to trespass upon my domain."

So he summoned his two messengers, the spirit of the
vineyard and the spirit of the meadow, and commanded
them to journey to the far end of the world. "There," said
he, "you will find a mountain with twin peaks. Beneath it
lies the realm of death, the domain of Mot. Lift up that
mountain upon your hands and descend. Be as the dead who
go down to the pit, and bring my word to Mot. But draw not
too close to his throne, lest he snatch you and devour you
like a lamb between his jaws. Keep your distance from him,
and thence proclaim what I say. Tell him that his proper
domains are the darkling depth below and the torrid deserts
above, and there he must stay!"

When Mot received this message he flew into a towering
rage. "Ho, ho!" he screamed. "So Baal is to sit on his throne
in ease and comfort, wrapped in the garment of heaven,
while I am to stay down here in the murk and the gloom, eating mud and drinking filth? Go, tell your master that if he
won't have *me* as his guest I will have *him!* Let him come
down here, and I will gladly regale him! I will heap upon him
such fare as he has never tasted before!"

Thereupon the messengers returned to Baal and repeated
the words of Mot. Then Baal was filled with fear.

"Nay," he cried, "I dare not go down! For Mot is waiting

with jaws agape, and he will surely gobble me up. Maybe he will be appeased if I send him rich fare to eat and rare wines to drink!"

So again he summoned his messengers, and this time he bade them take down to Mot lavish gifts of viands and drinks. "Flatter him and win his favor," he said. "Tell him that Baal is his servant, his devoted slave!"

But when Mot saw that his rival was trying merely to buy him off and was afraid to meet him face to face, he grew even more incensed than before and began to heap scorn upon Baal. "So your master is scared?" he stormed as the messengers approached him. "So Baal is trying to insult me? Tell him to show his mettle and come down. I desire not his gifts."

Then Baal saw that all his devices were vain and that now he must indeed confront his rival. So he made ready his chariot and took with him his clouds and his winds and his rains, and rallied his servitors and henchmen to his side, and bedaubed himself with red ocher as a charm against the forces of death, and went down into the world below to partake of the feast to which Mot had invited him.

But Baal had forgotten that whoever tastes of the food of death can return no more to the world of men; and no sooner had he put the bread to his lips than he was the prisoner of Mot, trapped in the darkling realm.

At once the earth began to languish, for no rain fell upon it and no green thing grew up; and presently two messengers appeared in heaven, breathless and distraught, and bowed themselves low before the throne of God.

"Sire," they cried, "we were down upon earth and we came to the haunts of Baal—the beautiful, verdant meads; but lo, he was nowhere to be seen! Baal has sunk into the world below!"

Thereupon God came down from his throne and sat upon the footstool, and down from the footstool and sat upon the ground, and he strewed ashes upon his head and put off his kingly robes and donned the garb of mourners. Then he roamed over hill and dale, tearing his flesh and crying in a loud voice, "Baal is dead!"

When the maiden Anat heard these words she was beside herself with grief. Like a cow bereft of its calf, or a ewe of its lamb, she wandered over hill and dale in search of her brother, tearing her flesh and crying in a loud voice, "Baal is dead!" At length, in the hour of the evening twilight, she came upon the sun at the moment when it was about to descend for the night into the world below.

"Lady Sun," she cried, "you alone of all the gods can go down into the world below and return therefrom. I beseech you, when next you come back, bring with you my brother Baal and load him upon my shoulders, that I may carry him up to the Mountain of the North and give him due burial in holy ground."

And the sun had compassion upon Anat, and when she returned at daybreak from the world below she brought with her the body of Baal and loaded it upon the shoulders of Anat; and together the two goddesses went up to the Mountain of the North, and they raised a loud keening and slaughtered many beasts in preparation for the funeral of Baal.

Then Anat came before the presence of God, where all the family of heaven was assembled, and she lifted her voice and wept. "How can you now make merry," she cried, "O queen and family of heaven? For behold, the mighty Baal is dead; His Highness the King of the Earth is no more!"

But now that he knew for certain what had passed, God would give way no more to helpless sorrow, and at once he turned to his consort. "Asherat," said he, "since Baal is dead we must appoint a successor. Name some other of your sons, and I will make him king of the earth!"

"But let us make sure," replied the queen, "that we appoint not one who will grow too big and hold us in contempt!"

"Well spoken," rejoined her consort. "But let us make sure no less that we appoint not a weakling. Whoever we choose must at least be as swift as was Baal in the chase and as nimble as he in poising the spear, and no less comely and fair!"

For a moment Asherat was lost in thought. Then she looked up, and there was a strange light in her eyes. "Maybe it were best," she said, "if after all we gave the kingship to Ashtar. He is a doughty youth, to be sure. Let Ashtar be king!"

So Ashtar went up to the throne of Baal to take his place as king of the earth and master of the gods. But when he sat upon the royal seat, his head did not even reach to its top, nor his feet to the footstool, for he was but a child. Howbeit, although he was too small to sit upon the throne of Baal in the Mountain of the North, Ashtar went down to earth and there reigned as king.

Meanwhile Anat kept roaming the earth, hunting the foeman of Baal, who had lured him down to the world below. At last, after many months, she came upon Mot strolling at leisure among the meadows. "Now," thought she, "I will trap him, for he does not know that I have already retrieved my brother from his murky domain." So she grasped the hem of his robe and began to entreat him. "Mot," she pleaded, "give back my brother!"

But Mot merely shrugged his shoulders. "Let me go," he replied. "What do you want of *me?* I am here to take the air and enjoy the countryside. But," he added darkly, "since you mention that brother of yours, I may as well warn you that, if ever I run into him, I will gobble him up!"

Anat said nothing, but proceeded on her way. For days and months she wandered over hill and dale, and all the while she was like a cow bereft of its calf, or a ewe of its lamb. At length she again encountered Mot strolling at leisure among the meadows. But now she lost no time in talk. Grasping him roughly by the shoulder, she ripped him up with her sword and burned his flesh in fire, and placed the morsels in a winnowing-fan, and ground them in a mill, and then sowed them into the earth. . . .

That night Anat had a strange dream. It seemed as though the beds of the rivers, which for months had been dry, were suddenly filled with honey, while down from the heavens poured a shower not of rain but of oil. When she awoke Anat knew that the dream was a sign, and straightway she went to God and related it to him. "Now am I certain," she said, "that Baal, after all, is alive, and that it was no dead body that I brought up for burial upon the Holy Hill. Baal has surely revived and has gone down from the mountain and is somewhere on earth!"

At these words God was filled with joy, and at once he

sent for the sun and bade her on her daily journey look out for Baal.

Meanwhile Baal had indeed revived and gone down to earth, and now he determined to settle accounts with Ashtar, who was presuming to reign in his stead. So he took his bludgeon and smote Ashtar roundly until he fell. Then he returned to the Mountain of the North and seated himself once more upon his royal throne. . . .

For six years Baal sat upon his throne in peace. But in the seventh year a strange thing occurred. All of a sudden the several parts of Mot's flesh, which Anat had so carefully sown into the earth, began to sprout up, and presently they were joined together once more, and the god arose again in his ancient form and might and challenged Baal to combat.

" 'Twas on your account," he cried, "that I was put to shame and ripped up by the sword and burned in fire and ground in a mill and sown into the fields. At last my luck has turned, and now it is *I* who will feed on *you!*"

But Baal rallied his henchmen and gave battle, and soon all the forces of Mot lay prone at his feet. Nevertheless, Mot himself remained undaunted and charged in fury upon his foe. Long and fierce was the battle, as they pranced like antelopes and gored like bulls and charged like stallions and stung like asps; and now Mot triumphed, and now Baal.

But all of a sudden, when the battle was at its height, the sun espied them from on high and called out to Mot from heaven and bade him give in. "How dare you fight against Baal?" she cried. "Beware lest God hear of your deed! For he will surely pluck up the mainstays of your dwelling, and your royal throne will be overturned and your scepter broken in sunder!"

At these words Mot was sore afraid. "Let Baal be king!" he gasped, rising from the ground whither he had been thrust. "Let Baal take the throne!"

So Baal returned to his palace and sat in state upon his throne. Then he called for the sun.

"Lady Sun," he proclaimed, "you shall have your reward. You shall eat the bread of aggrandizement and drink the wine of favor! You shall bear sway both above and below; gods and men alike shall bear witness to your power! Whenever you wander abroad Sir Adroit-and-Cunning shall be at your side, to be your escort and companion; and even as he helped to overcome the dragon and to thrust him back into the sea, so shall he help you whenever the dragon of heaven pursues you to your hurt!"

Then all the gods forgathered once more to do homage to Baal. Fatlings were slaughtered, and huge flagons set before him—flagons such as never housewife saw, holding each ten thousand cups of drink; and as he ate and drank a sweet-voiced stripling stood beside him, chanting songs for his delight and plying the cymbals.

Anat, however, was in no mood for merriment. "If," thought she, "Baal chooses to entertain the gods, there is nonetheless an account to settle with men, for during the time when he was absent from the earth they were quite ready to give their devotion to Ashtar and Mot." So when evening came she locked the gates of her mansion and stalked abroad on a wild rampage of vengeance. High and low, east and west, on the heights of the mountains and in the depths of the valleys, she cut down all she met, until presently she was wading to the hips in blood. But still she was not satisfied, and when at last she returned to her abode her mind was so filled with thoughts of carnage that the very furnishings of the house seemed, in the darkness, to take on human shapes and, waving her hands wildly, she lunged at the tables and chairs and footstools, overturning them in her mad onset and hacking them to pieces with her sword. It was, indeed, as though she were hewing down whole armies of assailants, and as the oil flowed from the overturned vessels and coursed in rivulets upon the floor, it seemed as though she were wading in pools of blood.

At last the first flush of daylight streaked the sky, and Anat came forth from the palace and bathed in the morning dew and put on clean raiment and scented herself with costly perfumes.

When Baal awoke and set eyes upon the scene he was greatly perturbed. "I am now at peace," he thought. "My kingdom is secure, and my wives dwell beside me, safe and sound. But Anat, it seems, is still bent on revenge, and the thought of battle is still in her mind."

So he summoned his two messengers. "Go unto Anat," he said. "Bow down before her and tell her that the time of warfare is past, for Baal is about to bring in upon earth an age of peace and goodwill. Bid her put aside her fury. Let her no longer weave plots and wiles, but rather a web of love to enmesh mankind. Bid her also come hither with all speed, for lo, I am minded to reveal my power from the Holy Hill."

Thereupon the messengers went forth with all dispatch. But as soon as Anat saw them approaching she was filled with alarm. "Behold," said she to herself, "some new foe has risen up against Baal, and he has sent to entreat my aid." And even before the envoys could utter a word she lifted her voice in a wild and savage song of war. And this is what she sang:

> "What foe is he who dares defy
> The God Who Chariots o'er the Sky?
> Let all take heed, who would assay
> The power of Baal and his sway!
>
> Although God's chosen one was he,
> I crushed the master of the sea.
> Lord High and Mighty was he hight;
> I made an end of all his might!
>
> The seven-headed monster too,
> The wily dragon—him I slew.
> His jaws were gaping for the feast;
> I put the muzzle on that beast!
>
> Unruly creatures all I bound,
> The frisking calf, the gruesome hound;
> The creeping serpent, foul and fell,
> Him I overthrew as well.
>
> So will I conquer all who strive
> My Baal from his throne to drive,
> Who raise against his rule their hand
> Or stop their ears at his command.
>
> Lo, I will fight them, might and main,
> And seize the plunder once again!"

When they heard these words the messengers of Baal were indeed amazed. But in a moment they had recovered themselves and, after making obeisance to her, they assured her that no enemy had risen against Baal and they told her that they were come to deliver in his name a message of glad tidings. And therewith they answered her savage words with a song of their own, rehearsing to her the pronouncement of Baal. And this is what they sang:

> "The word of mighty Baal do thou hear,
> The speech of Him Who Rides across the Clouds:
>
> 'Now do thou banish warfare from the earth,
> And love do thou implant within the land!
> Now do thou weave no longer on the earth
> Tissues of hate, but rather threads of peace;
> I bid thee, twine no longer in the land
> A mesh of guile, but rather skeins of love!
>
> Now haste, now hurry, now bestir thyself,
> And let thy feet come speeding unto me,
> Yea, let thy steps now haste to where I am.
> For there's a rede which I would rede to thee,
> A word which I would fain relate to thee.
> That word it is which windswept trees repeat,
> Which pebbles in the whisp'ring brooks rehearse,
> Which, like the murmur of a threnody,
> Heaven repeats to earth, and deeps to stars.
>
> Lo, I, installed as godhead of the north,
> Will fashion now upon that hill of mine
> A lightning such as heaven never knew,

A voice the like of which men never heard,
Greater than all mankind yet understand.

Come thou, and I, even I, will light my flame
Upon that holy place which evermore
Shall be the hill of mine inheritance,
Upon that lovely place which evermore
Shall be the mount where my puissance rests!' "

No sooner did she hear these words than Anat's heart was at once appeased, and in less time than it takes to tell she had joined the envoys and the three of them were winging their way to the Holy Hill.

When they reached the foot of the hill a wondrous sight met their eyes, for the whole sky seemed to be aflame, and every moment the clouds were rent with brilliant flashes of lightning, and deep peals of thunder echoed from crag to crag. Then Anat knew that Baal indeed was king; for the heavens declared his glory, and the firmament showed forth his handiwork.

Comment

This story is primarily a nature myth. Baal represents the power of the rains, Yam that of the sea and rivers, Mot that of the desert and the nether regions. In Arabic rain-watered soil is still called "land of Baal," while arid and barren places are known as *mawāt,* or "dead land"—a word cognate with the name Mot. As for Ashtar, who twice aspires to lordship of the earth and twice fails to qualify for that office, he is the power of artificial irrigation;

soil so watered is known in Arabic as 'athtarī, which is a form of the same word.

What the story relates, therefore, is the alternation of the seasons in the Syro-Palestinian year. First, toward the end of September, there is a struggle between rain and river as to who is rightfully the lord of the earth, lordship being determined in Oriental law by the fact of watering and quickening it. Then, when the river has been curbed and the power of Rain is supreme, the latter is in turn challenged—toward the end of May—by the power of Drought, who lures him into the underworld and himself reigns on earth during the summer months. Finally, with a display of lightning and electric storms, Rain returns and reclaims the throne—i.e., the drought breaks, and the cycle begins anew.

It is possible that in its original form this story was designed for an autumnal festival which marked the return of the rainy season and the beginning of the agricultural year. That festival would have been a Canaanite forerunner of the Hebrew Feast of Ingathering, still observed by Jews as the Feast of Booths. In accordance with a pattern common in the religions of the ancient Near East, the king would then have been temporarily deposed and subsequently reinstated in a special palace or pavilion, this procedure symbolizing the temporary eclipse and renewal of his people's corporate life. The purpose of the story would have been to interpret this ritual in universal terms—the king being translated into a god—and its various episodes would thus reflect or "project" the religious proceedings. On this basis, for example, the removal of Baal and the temporary occupancy of his throne by Ashtar would reflect or project the common primitive custom of appointing an "interim king" (*interrex*) during the last days of the year, when the normal lease of life is thought to have expired and the next one not yet to have commenced. Similarly, the building of the palace for Baal would reflect or project the construction of the special pavilion for the king—a feature which is likewise reproduced in the Babylonian "War of the Gods" (see p. 66). So, too, the lengthy discussion of the point whether or not the palace should have windows, and the explanation that they would ensure a regular supply of rain (see p. 216), would reflect or project the fact that the primary need at this season was to ensure adequate rainfall during the coming year.

Against the broad background of the seasonal pattern, however, the story develops along its own lines and incorporates several familiar themes of folklore which call for comment and explanation.

When Baal fights Yam he has to be equipped with two special bludgeons made for him by the divine smith. This recurs in an Egyptian myth relating how Horus fought Set, for there we are told that Horus was provided with a special weapon made by Ptah, the artisan of the gods. Similarly, in Vedic myth, when Indra engages the sinuous Vritra, he is equipped with a "whizzing bolt" especially fashioned by the artist Tvashtri. It is generally agreed by mythologists that these weapons represent the thunderbolt. Moreover, since the bludgeons are said (in the original text) to *"spring* from the hand of Baal," and since he was obviously provided with them in order to avoid the perils of a hand-to-hand encounter with the dragon, it is not improbable that they were regarded as magical weapons which, like Thor's hammer, had the power of returning automatically to their wielder if they failed to find their mark. This idea is by no means uncommon in folk tales (D 1094).

Again, when Ashtar is named to succeed the ousted Baal he fails to qualify because he is physically too small to occupy the latter's throne. He has therefore to be content with a limited sway on earth in place of kingship in heaven. There is a subtle point in this, for among ancient and primitive peoples a primary requisite for kingship is that the person who aspires to it must be taller than everyone else. Of Saul, for example, it is said distinctly that he was chosen to be king of Israel by reason of his "countenance and the tallness of his stature" (I Samuel 16:7); while Herodotus relates that Xerxes was the tallest of all the Persians.

It is also laid down that the successor of Baal must be "no less comely and fair," and that he must be nimble and strong. This too is a condition of kingship among primitive peoples. Thus before his installation the king of Konde is kept under strict surveillance to make sure that he is not a weakling who would become a men- ace to the land; while among the Varozwe (a Shona tribe) the absence of bodily blemishes was considered absolutely neces- sary in the occupant of the throne. The reason is, of course, that the king personifies and epitomizes the corporate life of his peo- ple. This explains the custom in many parts of the world of putting him to death as soon as he shows signs of sickness or old age (see pp. 205–206).

Baal's descent to the netherworld likewise plays on popular lore. The point lies in the common belief that anyone who eats the bread of that realm—or, alternatively, of fairyland—cannot return to the world of men (C 211). Persephone, for instance, is induced, while in Hades, to eat the seeds of a pomegranate in order to prevent her return to earth. Similarly, in Shinto myth, the pri- meval goddess Izanami eats of the food of the "Land of Yomi" after her death, and this prevents her husband Izanagi from bring- ing her back; while in the Finnish Kalevala the hero Wäinämöinen refuses for this reason to partake of drink in the land of Manala. The same belief also obtains among primitive peoples at the pres- ent day: the Zulus and Amatongas of South Africa hold that if the spirit of the dead touches food in the netherworld it can never come back to earth. Mot, excluded from the banquet tendered by Baal, gets his revenge by inviting his imprudent rival to break bread with *him* in the nether regions!

To reach Mot, Baal's messengers have to journey to a remote twin-peaked mountain in the farthermost north. The original text says only that they travel to "the mountain Tarkhuzziza and the mountain Sharrumagi." No such mountains are known, but Tarkhu and Sharruma are the names of deities worshiped in Asia Minor—i.e., in the land north of Canaan. Hence what we have here is another example of the familiar idea that demons live in the north, in the farthermost climes of the world (G 633). This belief is attested among the ancient Iranians, the Mandaeans, the Indians, the Jews, the Greeks, and many other peoples. Moreover, a survival of it may be detected even in English poetry; for in Milton's *Paradise Lost* the rebel angels are said to assemble in the north, while in the First Part of Shakespeare's *Henry the Sixth,* La Pucelle invokes the aid of spirits "under the lordly monarch of the north."

When Mot issues his invitation to Baal he complains that while *he* is expected to live in the netherworld, feeding on dirt and mud, his rival sits at ease, "wrapped in the garment of heaven." Here again we have the notion that the sky is a robe in which God is enfolded. The idea will be familiar to most readers from the Psalmist's address to God as one "Who coverest thyself with light as with a garment, stretchest out the heavens like a curtain" (Psalm 104:2). Similarly, in an ancient Iranian hymn, the god Mazda is said to "take heaven to himself as a garment, star-embroidered, gold-woven"; while Nonnus, a Greek poet of the sixth century A.D., describes "Heracles (i.e., Baal) of Tyre" as wearing "a star-spangled jerkin" and as being wrapped in a garment which lights up the skies at night. Odin too is said to wear an azure mantle representing the sky.

The imminent return of Baal is revealed to his sister Anat in a dream wherein she beholds the dry beds of the rivers suddenly filled with honey, the while oil pours down from heaven. This, in popular lore, is the typical description both of the Golden Age and of the Earthly Paradise (F 162.2.3). Indeed, it is specifically with reference to the latter idea that the Promised Land is portrayed in the Bible as a land "flowing with milk and honey"; while in Celtic legend the god Manannan praises the Isle of Man as being a place "where rivers pour forth a stream of honey." In the same way, too, the Greek poet Euripides says that when Dionysus first revealed himself to men "the rivers ran with honey."

Lastly, when the Lady Sun is commended by Baal for her intervention on his behalf, she is assured that henceforth she will have as her escort that same Sir Adroit-and-Cunning who formerly helped to hurl the dragon into the sea. The point of these words lies in the ancient belief that eclipses of the sun and moon are caused by the ravages of a celestial dragon who pursues them and swallows them (A 737.1). Thus in Indic belief it is the dragon Rahu or Svarbahnu who periodically gobbles them up, while in the Confucian classic *Tsun Tsiu* ("Springs and Autumns") the word "eat" is employed to describe the eclipse of April 20, 610 B.C. Similarly, in Scandinavian lore the sun is believed to be pursued constantly by a wolf named Skoll, while the Tatar tribe of Chuwashes uses the phrase "a demon has eaten it" to denote an eclipse of the sun. South of Lake Bakal it is asserted that the king of hell tries to swallow the moon, and in Jewish folklore a great fish is said to prey on the sun. It is, then, from such a fate that Baal promises to deliver the sun-goddess.

It should perhaps be added that, while the main portion of this story is contained on the clay tablets unearthed at Ras Shamra-Ugarit in Syria, a large gap has here been supplied from a fragmentary Egyptian papyrus, dating between 1550 and 1200 B.C., now in the Morgan collection in New York. This document, known as the Astarte Papyrus, appears to be part of an Egyptianized version of the tale, covering the incidents of Yam's initial oppression of the gods, his insult to Astarte, and Baal's spirited intervention. The supplement is necessary to give sequence and coherence to the narrative.

INDEX OF MOTIFS

(Numbers in parentheses refer to the standard classification in Stith Thompson's *Motif-Index of Folk-Literature*.)

Cross-Index